MARRIAGE — GROUNDS FOR DIVORCE

MARRIAGE — GROUNDS FOR DIVORCE

By

MONTE VANTON

LIBRARY OF CONGRESS CATALOG CARD NUMBER:
77-86320
ISBN 0-931024-01-3
VICTORIA PRESS/BURBANK, CALIFORNIA

TO MY SON
TOREN MICHAEL VANTON
AND CHILDREN FROM BROKEN HOMES
EVERYWHERE.

MADAME! YOU ARE NOT MY EQUAL
WITH YOUR GOSSAMER FILAMENTS,
YOU ARE MY SUPERIOR!
BUT, WHEN YOU USE HEMP
I SCORN YOU . . . .

ACKNOWLEDGMENTS

I would like to thank all those friends who gave so much of their time, enthusiasm and assistance in the preparation of the book for publication. E. Joseph Cossman of Palm Springs, California, a tower of strength and support. My editor, Pat Murphy of Victoria, B.C., with whom, so many times, I rolled and wrestled on the floor of my living room while we battled over the syntax, style and repetition in the manuscript. Pat, huge and loud as a bear, but deep down, soft and gentle as a child. Ed Gould, columnist and author, who taught me how to "sculpture." Len Gibbs, one of Canada's leading artists, for his jacket design. Jan Gould, who read the completed manuscript and showed me where it was NOT completed. And finally to two English gentlemen whose memories I treasure. Samuel Morris Rich, author, teacher and mentor in my final year in school (7th grade), who, although forever bearing down on me with his thick red pencil, lit the spark and fanned the flames, even though I was destined to do all my head work, upon leaving school, in a barber shop in London. And Simon Elvis, gentleman, aristocrat and portrait painter to Her Majesty, Queen Elizabeth II who urged the slum kid from the East-end of London, armed with a grade school education to "WRITE!"

TABLE OF CONTENTS

MARRIAGE — GROUNDS FOR DIVORCE

" . . . . whenever in the history of civilization women have ceased to be an economic (domestic) asset in marriage, marriage has decayed; and sometimes civilization has decayed with it." *Will Durant —* *'THE STORY OF CIVILIZATION.'*

INTRODUCTION

Why an Introduction? Is it to introduce the author, the book and its contents, or does it offer itself as a synopsis of the material within?

Sometimes I skip the introduction when I am impatient to get into the book. In fact, for me, the success of a book is determined by whether or not I read the introduction when I finish the book.

Perhaps the introduction should be placed at the end of a book. By this time you either hate the author, love him, or are indifferent. If you love him, you know him and share in his essential nature. You are interested in his motivation for the book and its gestation.

Let me say at the outset, that this is neither a HOW TO book, nor a text. The author is neither a sociologist nor a psychiatrist and there are no case histories within. The writer is an ordinary man, like you — someone who jostles you in the subway, in the street or on the bus. In fact you might be tempted to say: "Why, I could have written that myself!"

Many books written on serious subjects such as religion, sex, behavioral psychology, human relations, marriage and divorce are devoured by millions all seeking the better life. Many of these works claim to have the solution to all human problems.

This is not the purpose of this book. No one book could answer every person's problems.

My inquiry into divorce covers many aspects of our daily life, our culture, our historical background, our sexual mores, drives, hopes and fears. It may be said that at times, I contradict myself and this may be true. There are many different people with as many different problems. No one thesis could ever presume to offer the solutions to all marital ills.

I hope that each reader will find a parallel with his own unique circumstances in some of the thoughts I express, that he may be sparked to search deeper within himself for the answer which is right for him.

I began writing this book early in 1962 and finished it in 1965, before the emergence of the women's liberation movement and the Berkeley revolt. America still slumbered in the post-McCarthy period. University students expressed their radical concern for social reform by swallowing goldfish, embarking upon perilous pantyraids in women's dorms and stuffing themselves, by the dozen, into telephone booths. President Kennedy had just been elected, and people were vaguely aware of "advisors" being sent to Viet Nam — Viet What?

Consumerism filled our lives. The bug had not yet challenged America's great love affair; there were Communists in every pumpkin patch and under every mattress. And our land was the home of plenty, virtue, apple-pie, motherhood — and a disastrous divorce rate!

For personal reasons, the book remained unpublished until this year and, while some changes in the divorce laws have taken place in the interval, the monumental problems afflicting marriage and the post-divorce period still remain. The divorce rate continues to climb. I believe it reached 70 percent in Southern California a few years ago. Many divorced parents today were children of broken homes at the time I began writing this book.

The legal changes referred to here are as effective as a chain link fence in containing an advancing glacier. Our greatest national problem swells and feeds upon itself and grows more ominous daily.

The founders of the women's liberation movement and I developed our opposing philosophies at about the same time. I hadn't heard of women's liberation in 1962 but, as these pages will reveal, I felt strongly that one of the main causes of the break down in marriage was the incredible freedom and dominance enjoyed even then by the American woman. Her rights, privileges, status and protection in law, contrasted with that of her European and Japanese sisters, marked her as the most liberated woman in history. Yet marriage, as a way of life, was cracking up and women demanded still more freedom.

My first awareness of this new militancy occurred when I was into the third chapter of the book. I heard on a radio broadcast, Betty Friedan discussing her new book, "The Feminine Mystique." I listened in amazement and shock. *The bank robber was demanding bigger and better banks to rob!*

In the ensuing pages I say about marriage: "We are out of one era, and not yet arrived at the new one." I also say that it appears that females, before marriage, train themselves to be self-sufficient for the post-divorce period. This, I believe, is another important cause of the erosion of marriage. For what prospect of success would the crew of a ship have of arriving safely in port were they to spend all their time learning and practicing life boat drill and swimming?

Few voices are raised against the Women's Liberation movement: The whole nation pays lip service to the cause. Men may blanch and wince, but discretion is safer. Little comment is made on the spectacle of women's liberationists fighting among themselves, frequently with more passion than they employ opposing the injustices of a man's world. Unchallenged, too, is the fact that many women, confused and frustrated, use the movement as an outlet for deep-rooted angers which, in all likelihood, have their origins in early childhood.

Women demand greater rights and freedoms — to be better

mothers and wives? No! To be equal with men! Out of one era and not yet arrived at the next, women campaign not to make marriages and motherhood more fruitful and successful, but to render their present mid-stream twilight zone more bearable. Tragically, their success in this endeavor guarantees them more anger, frustration and bitterness.

My apostasy when I embarked upon this book was a lonely one. Today, I am delighted to see I am being joined by a growing army, not of men but of women, in many parts of America. They call themselves "Fascinating Womanhood," and their ambition is to grow as wives and mothers, to cater to their husbands, and support them in marriage and in their manhood, to provide their children with the joy of a LOVING mother, who is truly with them, and to make their homes havens of happiness, health and comfort. And then — if there is time left over, to enrich their minds with the treasures offered by schools, and universities, not for degrees, and extra income, but for personal growth.

Several years ago, the State of California, alarmed by the spiralling divorce rate, authorized studies of this problem. A report was compiled by a select group of lawyers and jurists and, as a result, a new day dawned in the shape of a few changes in the divorce laws. One of these new laws substituted the term "dissolution of marriage" for the ugly word "divorce." This was a major break-through! Since divorce cases are handled by lawyers in the framework of the rules of the Court and, since most divorce actions were brought by women, the plaintiffs, then by extension, the husband was the defendant — the criminal. Today, happily, the husband need no longer regard himself as a felon. We now have a new word for divorce — but, divorce, unmindful of this brave new word, continues on in unabated fury.

In England, the ugly word "strike" is softly termed "industrial dispute." But the recent "industrial dispute" affecting England's miners and coal industry almost smashed the nation's economy!

In 1962, the Supreme Court of the United States made its historic decision affecting the American Negro, which gave rise to Selma and ugly confrontations in the South. At that time I proposed, with regard to the epidemic of divorce, that huge masses of people would have to influence Congress to enact revolutionary new laws to cure this problem or — Congress would have to independently create such laws which would in time bring about the enormous changes in our thinking and cultural habits needed to cure this national illness. I prophesied that the havoc being wrought in the South, the refusals of Governors, Faubus, Wallace and Maxton of Georgia to obey this new law — who inflamed an incendiary, Negro-hating and frightened white population, would eventually change and give way to adjustment and acceptance. Today, the American Negro has advanced more in the last 14 years, socially, politically, culturally and economically, than he has done before in the history of the republic. A Negro congresswoman delivers one of the keynote addresses at the 1976 Democratic convention and receives a tumultuous ovation. A Southerner, overwhelmingly supported by Negroes is elected by acclamation as the Democratic presidential nominee. The closing prayer of the convention is delivered by Martin Luther King Sr. And the vast auditorium is filled by the Negro freedom song "We Shall Overcome." Blacks and whites stand hand in hand, eyes brimming with tears of joy as this anthem swells through Madison Square Garden. This is America? 1976? And all in so short a space of time!

No less than the above great Negro triumph must be achieved in the national marital holocaust. But it will take similar revolutionary new laws, or a vast public outcry to bring about such laws.

Today, some 11 years after I wrote the chapter "Custody — A Matter of Gender?," Canada is taking a long look at who is the most suitable custodial parent in divorce. Things are changing, but oh, so slowly.

The spill-over of the divorce plague of California threatens the whole of the United States and Canada. For, it appears that the life style of California is so pervasive, that how California goes, so goes America — and as America goes, so goes the rest of the world. As far away as Japan, a country where, until recently, divorce was unheard of, this disease is growing at an alarming rate. Before 1957, coincidentally the year that saw the first female elected to the Japanese Diet, marriages were traditionally arranged by the parents of the betrothed. Today, being "in love" becomes the prime mover of the union. Parents who try to intervene are viewed with a similar antipathy experienced by American parents 50 years ago. Materialism, consumerism and like education for both sexes all contribute to the rising incidence of Japanese divorce. A tradition of 2000 years is beginning to die.

It is Mr. and Mrs. Everyman who suffer from the growing disease of divorce. It is Mr. and Mrs. Everyman who, in the loneliness of their silent rooms at night, wonder: "Where did I go wrong? How can I prevent it from happening again?" And therefore, it is Mr. Everyman who has attempted to seek an answer to this problem affecting so many Americans today.

If the answer could be found in the collective knowledge of judges, doctors, lawyers, legislators, sociologists and professors, the problem would have been licked long ago. Sadly it is not and the sickness grows more virulent every day.

In no other area in our national life do we make so many mistakes as before, during and after marriage. There has never been a time in history where so many people blithely continued the same foredoomed behavior pattern — even to the point of handing down these formulas to their offspring without any attempt to question, analyze and search for a solution to prevent these mistakes in the future.

Several of my friends, on hearing the title of my book have suggested that perhaps I am cynical in such a choice. Nothing could be further from the truth. The title evolved from a simple, mathematical, logical deduction!

Several years ago, when visiting my soon-to-be ex-wife, I spent a few moments talking to my next door neighbor. It was a lovely summer evening, the crickets were merrily chirping and the air was filled with a sweet, spicy fragrance. The moon cast a gentle glow and had it not been for the stark drama about to be played, one could have said: "God's in His Heaven, all's right with the world."

Coincidentally, my neighbor, a professor of law at the University of California, was also going through a divorce.

Neither of us had chosen this ordeal; we had both been given our marching orders within weeks of each other. We had purchased our homes at about the same time and had dwelt within them a scant two months.

We had tended our gardens, planted trees and flowers, and now in the midst of our blossoming efforts, were consoling each other and asking: "What went wrong?"

The charges brought against my friend and I by our respective wives were "mental cruelty." And we were wondering how on earth could a man avoid such a charge during marriage.

Now here was a professor of law at my side. I surely would learn from him. But he was as baffled as I. He told me that Mental Cruelty could run all the way from looking crossly at your wife to having a night out with the boys!

"You mean," I said, "if a man, comes home after a pressure-ridden day at the office and is greeted with the news by his wife that her mother is coming for dinner and says 'Oh Hell!', that's mental cruelty?" He answered me, it could be construed that way! "You mean," I continued, "that if I have some disagreement with my wife, put my foot down on some particular subject, I am exposing myself to a possible charge of mental cruelty?" He sadly admitted that eventuality.

"But how," I argued, "can you go through a marriage and avoid all the human elements that cause disharmony, strife and disagreement? Why, marriage itself is conducive to all the ups and downs of daily living. In fact, two people, living closely together as they do in marriage are bound to have labor pains!" He knew of no way these pitfalls could be avoided.

I remained silent and baffled for a few moments. I refused to be beaten. "But, if any of these incidents that occur daily, weekly, in marriage can be deemed mental cruelty, and mental cruelty is grounds for divorce, then since marriage causes these so-called incidents — why — then marriage itself is grounds for divorce!"

I had now solved the problem. I had found my answer! This blinding revelation had an equally shattering effect on my friend as it did on me. After a few minutes of silence, we shook hands and went our own way — he to his divorce courts, I to mine. . . .

Were the women's liberation movement to achieve all the goals it seeks today, tomorrow there would be a new compilation of grievances. This revolution is a war that can never be won — for conquest spells failure.

Chapter 1

PANDORA

There's a small silver-framed photograph on my desk. Storks stand on either side of the frame, and at each corner, a bird of peace — doves — four in all. At the bottom, on one side, is a clock, on the other, a weighing machine. In the center is an inscription, "Arrived 8-31-57: weight 7 lbs. 4 ozs." At the top of the frame is inscribed "Toren Michael Vanton," and in the photograph a smiling little boy, eyes veiled with long lashes is perusing his very own book, the title of which, barely discernable, is: "When I grow —."

Tory is about to join the millions of children from broken homes. Tory, just three and a half, full of love, hell and mischief, unfolding each day into something more wonderful, is about to have his world shattered. The continuity and expectation of seeing father and mother daily, together, are fading. And the bewilderment that comes with seeing one parent at a time is beginning to emerge.

This rock, this firmament, is beginning to split. Can you accept it Tory without withdrawing inwardly? Can your world change so drastically and still not call upon you to seek security from your own fragile resources? I hope and pray you don't have to. For the resources of a little boy are so few that the very need to seek them inwardly guarantees the fear, confusion, and unresolved conflicts that can follow in later life.

I am sorry Tory. I wish I knew how to make amends, to redress this deficit in your world. I wish I knew the answers —.

I had always wanted a little boy like you, and you filled my greatest expectations. I looked forward to each new day, to each new word, each new accomplishment learned with such joy and glee. I anticipated the years ahead and saw you emerging — babyhood, boyhood, adolescent, teenager, man and father. Now I will not see the daily growth, year by year, but only the measured sections doled out to me through my "visitation rights." And if the pain of separation becomes too hard to bear I hope nature does not come to my rescue and harden my susceptibility to you.

Divorce. Ugly word, dread word. I do not share the Catholic attitude toward divorce, but I feel the relationship between husband and wife is as closely interwoven as that between parents to children. Yet it can be split asunder like any other legal bond.

Marriage. If this is so holy a state, so close a relationship, how come you arrive home one night, like any other night, snap your fingers and calmly announce: "I can't stand it anymore, I've seen my attorney, I am going to get a divorce."

What has happened to marriage? Daily one hears of people one knows who are about to be divorced. The numbers swell — "You know so and so, I hear they're getting divorced!" "No! So and So? I thought they were very happy."

The tempo increases as though the world was spinning faster on its axis, until you begin to count your friends and even the people you know casually, and find they are all getting into the divorce mill, or on the brink. And, while you are sorry and duly commiserate with your spouse, somehow you feel like the driver of a car who sees some other poor devil getting a ticket and glows smugly within because it isn't him. But a miss today is no guarantee forever. And I wonder how many of us commenting on the news that so and so is getting divorced, fail to recognize that, for us too, the sands are quickly running out.

Millions of people are being divorced! More than one could ever dream possible. Newspapers give scant attention to this typical feature of American life. Were we to widen our circle of friends 50 times over, we would be dumbfounded at the spectacle of our society splitting apart so rapidly. And of those not yet arrived at the finality of divorce, millions are approaching, through marital confusion and angry feelings of unfulfillment, the anteroom of unholy dismatrimony.

A gloomy picture? Yes! We in America have a strong distaste for unpleasant realities. We prefer the sugar-coated pill, the drug of television and the dreams of motion pictures. We hide our heads under the blankets, like children and blot out the awful truth. But the truth grows more awesome every day. How can we hope to stem this tide unless we rid ourselves of the "make me happy at any price" attitude and stop this cataclysm before we become a nation of men living apart from women, breeding in our dark confusion bewildered, unhappy, angry children.

It is time to take stock. We are indifferent because we think it's only happening to us and a few friends — it's happening to everybody. Will we calmly accept this situation or, shall we ask, "Why?"

Are we all basically sick? We probably have more marriage counselors, psychoanalysts, psychiatrists and psychologists, and more people visiting them than any other nation in the world. And — we have more divorces than any other nation in the world. I don't believe communism was ever our greatest menace — the threat to our survival as a nation is the state of our mental health and our overwhelming divorce rate.

We have more money, schools, food, clothes, automobiles, roads, houses, factories, churches, cults, jobs, savings, advertising, radio, TV and movies than any other nation in the world — and we're starving to death in marriage.

Perhaps if enough of us understood that our problems are so much alike, that one person's experience is actually the pattern of the whole, that what is guaranteed to happen to you will happen to me, that it is not just our spouses who are so impossible — they are very little different from other men and women — we will finally recognize that the answer does not lie in divorce. We might as a consequence acknowledge that marital strife will continue until we remove the conditions which, like a miasma, are poisoning the very air of nearly all married couples, guaranteeing their marital doom.

If five hundred divorced couples met and each in turn described the faults of their ex-spouses, their joint confessions would resemble the single movement of a flock of birds wheeling and turning as one body.

In the first volume of "The Story of Civilization," Will Durant, one of America's great historians and philosophers, says: "Whenever, in the history of civilization, women have ceased to be an economic asset in marriage, marriage has decayed; and sometimes civilization has decayed with it." Durant was referring to early primitive societies, but its implications for modern America are ominous. The economic asset Durant alluded to was of a domestic nature, such as the nursing and rearing of children, the feeding of the family, the caring for the domestic animals, and with time left over, the tending of the kitchen garden.

I can just hear some of our emancipated females mutter, "Yes, and I bet their husbands didn't find them very sexy when they came home at night with their dirty nails and scraggy hair." I wager the males were lustier in those days than the husbands who wearily return at night, exhausted after a pressure-driven day, to their petulant, well-manicured and sexily clad wives. Our hero, seeking approval, a pat on the head drives himself into an early demise, which end he hastens by buying huge blocks of insurance — he bets he will die young — so his wife may continue comfortably when he is dead.

We have a crazed ambition to have more and more of the world's goods — bigger and newer cars, bigger and more expensive houses, more labor saving devices and more comfort. Each wife views the one slightly ahead as superior, and that one, in turn, views the one just ahead of her in home and jewelry with envy. And the one without, lives for the day when she can get started on this crazy ladder that goes nowhere. And the common complaint of many wives is: "I'm bored, I've nothing to do."

Our society has developed to the point where the female has "ceased to be an economic asset in marriage." And with this phenomenon we are witnessing the decay of marriage as an institution, as a fundamental, functioning social unit.

If Will Durant is right, then we are rushing headlong into disaster. No, we are there, we have arrived! What is so terribly wrong with us that we fail to see that the material things we strain to possess bring us, not fulfillment but emptiness. And the very things that would enrich and fulfill our lives we view with disdain? How did we get this way?

One of the most frequently heard complaints of wives is: "My husband is always tired when he comes home at night. He eats his dinner, watches T.V. and falls asleep." Another — "He never takes me anywhere. All he talks about is business. He's married to his work. There MUST be a better life than this."

This is all very shattering to the female ego, especially when she has husbanded her strength all day, manicured her nails, fixed her hair, watched her diet and done all the things the books prescribe on "how to be sexy." And her husband falls asleep.

Another complaint: "All my friends' husbands are buying their wives new cars and larger houses — why don't you show some backbone and get another job?"

The favorite gripe is, "You are fulfilled, you go to work, meet interesting people every day, I want to get a job . . ." Divorce Court.

Among the largest group of potential divorcees are middle class wives in the 32 to 40 age group. The desperate years approach. If sex is not going to reveal itself to them now, in all its wild rapturous splendor the novels and motion pictures have promised, it will be too late. Its now or never — Divorce!

Somehow things have turned around since I was a little boy in Wales. Divorce then was virtually unheard of. A divorced woman was avoided as though she had the plague. Her social structure was a little higher than a street walker. I admit things were a bit stiff in those days. Usually only the rich obtained divorces. We really didn't think the rich took their marriages too seriously — they were more interested in indulging themselves. If marriage interfered why — just go to court and end it. Easy come easy go. Somehow, the poor divorcee struck the public in a like manner — loose, easy virtue and no moral backbone.

With the adults of my childhood, marriage was sacred, inviolable, permanent and built to withstand shocks, storms, unemployment, wars, sickness and even the occasional infidelity and drunkenness. But in spite of so many difficulties, people lived their lives together, aiding and comforting each other, so each became complete.

And all this without automobiles and private homes. Most people lived in small flats or single rooms, shared common toilets and cooked over gas ring burners or wood-burning stoves. There were no refrigerators, deep freezers, or telephones. Frequently no electricity. Certainly there was little financial security and the loss of a job invariably spelt disaster for the family.

I do not pine for the "good old days," but why was marriage more successful when there were so few material goods and money, and so unsuccessful when we have so many possessions, ease and money? Is there a clue here?

I am tempted to believe there is. The attitude of the wealthy towards marriage in Britain before the last war, the rapid changing of partners — "I wonder if sex will be better with someone new?" The trumped up excuses — "He criticized me in public." — "We are not compatible," seems to be similar to the situation in our own country today.

The lack of earnestness and effort in marriage in America, excuses of "mental cruelty," pre-arranged adultery, incompatibility and criticism, reach across a wide range of years to the laissez faire attitude of the rich Englishman.

Throughout history, with rare short intervals, it has been a man's world and marriage has survived. This historical pattern changed temporarily in Rome in the first century B.C. Increasingly, the nation's work, including domestic, was performed by

slaves. Coincidentally, at this time, marriage began to disintegrate and the Roman women's lib movement was born. As
slaves became more plentiful, they assumed more and more
responsibilities in the running of the Roman household. The rich
Roman matron found herself with nothing to do — nor could
she do anything if she wanted to — she was untrained. So she
became clever at doing her hair, (when there wasn't a slave
around), dieting, selecting gowns and decorating her person.
She read Ovid and developed the art of attracting lovers to
overcome her listlessness and boredom.

The growth of her liberty did not increase her happiness,
rather it increased her resentment and accelerated her demands
for even more freedom. Roman women organized and petitioned
the Senate to enact more liberal laws favoring women. Livy,
quoting a famous speech of Cato, who deplored the Roman
female's desire for greater freedom, says at the conclusion of
this speech: `` . . . and to put them on an equality with their
husbands, do you imagine you will be able to bear them? From
the moment they become your equals they will become your
masters.''

Rome wallowed in luxury. Fewer and fewer Romans married.
The birth rate rapidly declined. Roman hegemony was
threatened. To stem this tide, the Roman Emperor Augustus,
issued severe edicts punishing those who abstained from marriage, and rewarding those citizens who married and bore
children.

There is much speculation about the causes that led to the
decline of the Roman power and its empire. The close knit
family unit is an integral part of a consolidated and successful
state. It follows that a disintegrating family unit must presage
the nation's decline.

The early patriarchs of Rome were stern, serious-minded
men, devoted to their homes and family gods. This strong
familial unit was symbolic of early Roman strength. The
majesty and sovereignty of Rome was celebrated right at the
family hearth, and the father, for better or worse, was the head
of the family.

Marital disintegration, previously unheard of, assumed epidemic proportions. Roman women, released from their economic contribution to the household, turned their energies to personal adornment and went outside the home to seek satisfactions and self-fulfillment. (Am I writing about Rome or modern America?)

It is often wondered whether the institution of marriage is a natural state or — the result of a power preconditioning inflicted upon mankind to plague and perplex him. This is by no means a recent thought. According to the earliest Greek writers, Hesiod and Homer, who lived at the close of the 8th century B.C. marriage was considered a punishment visited upon mankind through the wrath of Zeus. It appeared that Zeus had had it "up to here" with Prometheus. Prometheus, friend and patron of mankind, had twice deceived Zeus. First in giving man fire and subsequently by placing bones instead of meat in the fat wrapped offering to Zeus. Zeus naturally thought the fat contained meat and blew his stack when he discovered inedible bones. The punishment was to be the direst the Gatherer of Clouds could conceive. The verdict brought forth was — Woman. According to legend Pandora was the forerunner of the plague sent by Zeus to harass and confound a hitherto happy and contented mankind.

Certainly, there have been enough jokes and swipes taken at wives and marriage. As far back as Socrates, marriage was a subject for derision. The great philosopher was often sympathized with by his friends and admirers for putting up with a hell of a marriage and a shrew for a wife, and he, the most lovable and peaceful of humans.

Is it possible that wedlock is a system devised by the state to guarantee its continuity, stability and fruitfulness — and by the parents of female children to ensure their future and function? This all may seem to be unfair and one-sided, it is not to be denied, but, whenever one examines the pattern of nature out of context, she frequently appears to be cruel and one-sided.

Somehow, in our rush to become independent of household responsibilities, and in our hurry to enjoy the supposed rewards of a highly developed technology, we have lost sight of the basic pact. Like the English aristocracy and the decadent Romans we are rich in luxury and impoverished in marriage.

Marrying FOR LOVE is as foolhardy as going into the restaurant business because one enjoys eating. The pleasures of eating have nothing to do with a business as complicated as running a restaurant. And could, indeed, with all its attendant problems, ruin one's appetite for food.

Chapter 2

MARRY FOR LOVE?

Marriage has endured for thousands of years but love has lasted longer and, undoubtedly, will survive. But in no age have so many people merged the two and rushed headlong into wedlock because they were "in love."

This "marry for love" business is a comparatively recent innovation. It's older than radio and TV certainly, but not that much.

Up to the turn of the century, in nearly all nations, the serious and perplexing institution of marriage was arranged by sober-minded, mature people — the parents no less. Rarely was it brought about by the young people themselves. In some countries the bride and groom met for the first time at the altar.

Much discussion and bargaining took place before agreement was reached and contracts were signed. Regardless of whether the parents were peers, peasants, artisans or aristocrats, it was presumed the parents knew best. They should — they had been through it before.

And, to the wedding, the bride's parents brought a dowry, its size befitting their station in life. A wonderful idea this dowry for it gave the couple a firm foundation on which to build the marriage. Love was not considered a substitute.

However, custom demanded that if the husband returned the wife, he should also return the dowry. Fair enough.

In our Western Civilization, few dowries are given before marriage; *instead the wife gets one at its termination* in the form of home, half the estate, alimony and a mortgage on the

husband's future labors. I wonder how many marriages would
have taken place in former, happier days if there had been no
dowry but, in its stead, alimony and community property at the
conclusion of marriage.

Oh, there have been wonderful moments in history when
lovers defied their parents: Romeo and Juliet, Heloise and
Abelard, Cyrano and Roxanne. But curiously, these lives were
cut conveniently short. Suicide, murder and mayhem froze the
lovers in their rhapsody. They never tasted the joys of living
together for 10, 20 or 50 years. They never lost their beauty and
virility. Romance was with them always.

They were never bothered with in-laws, domesticity, diapers,
household chores, worrisome work and unemployment. They
died early and disappeared.

When these stories were written, they were cherished as they
are today — but with a difference. They were recited and
play-acted but everyone knew they were fiction. They were
dream stuff, beautiful and ennobling — but not life. Life was
something else again. It was work, home and children. Romantic love rarely existed in marriage (its place was outside the
home). There have always been love and lovers, but marriages
were arranged — and they endured.

Somewhere along the line we have taken what was meant as
fantasy and woven it into the fabric of our existence. ''In love''
becomes the cornerstone of modern marriage, and because it is
still fantasy, we build the marriage structure on quicksand.

We talk a lot about love, yet who can define the word? Is the
word equally applicable for God, country, father, mother,
sweetheart, children and wife? To some it means sex, to others
love is aesthetic — ethereal. Can it possibly be all these things?
In our Judeo-Christian culture lust and desire are equated with
the devil — the sin of Adam. And so we inheritors of the
Christian ethos carry our burden of guilt; our bodies, confused
and bewildered, made by God and . . . conditioned by religion.

This dilemma stems in part from two powerful forces opposing each other in the matter of love. Religion urges us to love each other and our neighbors as ourselves. Our bodies and feelings strive to oblige — but in their own way. The bewildered human animal gravitates from one side to the other, until he eventually steers a safe middle course — neither knowing or feeling. Eventually, this confusion manifests itself in different types of abnormalities and aberrations.

To the word "love" must be added another dimension "in love." To hear some women explain the precise differences between these two conditions, one would imagine that they alone had cornered all the wisdom on the subject. The ambition of most Western women is not only to be "in love" but to have it last forever.

"Love" is easily distinguishable from "in love." In the latter, sexual awareness is at its peak, immediate and urgent. The senses tingle, and the body feels good and alive; colors sparkle and the world glows; everything is a beautiful backdrop for a blissful state of mind. Meetings are adventures and partings are sad. Music and poetry are the languages of this enchantment. Most people have experienced this state and those who haven't hope to. It is their deepest desire.

One day it will happen — in a bus, on a plane, at the office, across a crowded room — suddenly and overwhelmingly.

Romanced in a thousand songs, books and films, whispered and talked about, longed for, dreamed about. Is it any wonder this high hope becomes the sole prerequisite for marriage? The approval which attends a marriage where the principals are "in love" makes the event a social triumph. Those whose turn has not yet come envy the lucky bride and groom and long for their day. And when a marriage takes place without the magic of "in love" present friends are confused and regretful. They whisper that the couple must have been disillusioned to have settled for so little, to have fallen so far short of the jack-pot.

Marry for love? Let us examine this incredible proposition and see if it is indeed the sole guarantor of marital success.

No business contract could ever contain enough clauses to

anticipate all the conditions and contingencies of a marriage. No partnership could ever sustain the close contact inherent in the circumstances of marriage. And certainly no business could endure where the executive roles were so ill-defined, the parties in competition, and where one party sustained the heaviest load.

And into this difficult contractual relationship enter the inexperienced young, often bereft of rational judgment. To be ''in love'' is to be intoxicated. A wonderful state but is this a time for careful thought and appraisal?

Is it a time to judge character, capabilities, strengths and weaknesses? At this exciting period pock-marks become beauty spots, imperfections disappear. Love is akin to madness — in fact it has often been called madness, Cupid's dreaded wound. The contract becomes even more tenuous when we realize the lovers only see each other on dates, when they are on their best behavior. Each encounter an adventure — no serious matters here. Is this a time for objectivity and cool assessment? Does one buy a steamship line because one enjoyed a short cruise?

Movies, parties, dances and walks in the moonlight — are these the testing grounds for marriage? Our lovers tell each other repeatedly how much they have in common, see eye to eye on everything, love to do the same things. And years later, on the threshold of divorce — have little in common, see eye to eye on nothing and hate doing the same things.

Song-writers, novelists, film-makers, and other distributors of pre-fab romance present this somnambulistic state as the single prerequisite for enduring marriage. And still this Cinderella state continues, despite the overwhelming evidence that this condition is the worst possible basis for marriage.

''One day I will meet a man and he will love me always. And he will be tender and passionate and desire me hourly, daily, . . . always.'' And, oh how heart-broken, cheated and disillusioned our bride is going to be when she finds out it is a lie — that her husband is not hungry for her morning, noon and night. That he, like other men, tires, becomes increasingly occupied with his work, grows fat and accepts love as a part, but only part, of his life. But the cooking and the dishwashing continue and the endless domestic chores go on forever. Is life passing her by?

But the myth continues . . . "I will love one man until I die." And the myth guarantees disappointment and conflict. And no one says "Stop! You are dreaming. You are living in a fantasy world." Marriage is tough, demanding and difficult. And one thing it ain't is a wild, never-ending love affair. Sex is always alluring when it is mysterious, coupled with difficulty of attainment. Certainly marriage does not further this lure.

There are few women, who in the final discussions with their husbands prior to divorce don't say, "I am just not in love with you anymore."

He: "You mean you don't love me?"

She: "Yes, of course I love you, but I am not 'in love' with you."

This statement is often followed by a bewildering dissertation on the precise difference between one feeling and the other.

Regardless of the condition of the marriage, husbands rarely seek divorce. It's the wife who ponders this cataclysmic step. After many fruitless discussions, she usually concludes with, "I have thought about this for a long time, my mind is made up." In reply to further pleas of her husband, she states with finality: "The feelings are gone, dead!"

The husband does not usually counter. It's too painful to challenge the edict. His pride and ego are dangerously threatened. He admits that it is true the urgency of sexual love has waned, the complexities of living have consumed more and more of his energy, but he's content, more or less, with the other rewards of marriage, the partnership, the children, the home and the building of something he considers worthwhile. And although romance has long since departed he sees no reason to end the marriage. But wives, at this point, are amazingly adamant. Men are astounded that their spouses can be so resolute — they would have capitulated long ago.

Husbands have said in desperation: "She's crazy! I swear she's mad" — or — "But, we were in love at one time, and it changed, how does she know the same won't occur again with another man. What will she do — go from man to man?"

To sustain romance, one should never marry the "in loved one." The erroneous premise which gave birth to marriage kills the marriage. "In love" was the start of marriage, "out of love" is the end.

Yet the dream continues. Mothers who have been through divorce do nothing to warn their daughters of this fallacy. They fondly hope their daughters will find the everlasting romance that they missed so that they too may enjoy this adventure vicariously. And women who have been through divorce cling tenaciously to the belief that they married the wrong man, but the next will be Mr. Right!

I believe, in spite of what I have written, it is possible to fall in love and have a wonderful marriage, but I also believe there are very few of us who can achieve this happiness from this chimeric starting point.

We haven't developed the wisdom and the stability to bring this about, nor can we as long as we hold firm to the ambition that the "in love" state is the only cementing bond of marriage.

I believe, in some magical way, God blessed mankind by giving him the gift of love. But in this design, man was only given a taste, a sample of a potential supreme joy. No effort, no work, no experience required. Suddenly, from out nowhere, a wand is waved and you are "in love."

Man is given a glimpse of the promised land, but it is only a glimpse of the bliss that lies beyond.

That rare lucky couple, starting at this point and realizing that this state will not last forever, begins immediately to work with zeal and unselfish effort toward building a solid foundation for the love that will follow once the "free ride" is over. Using this *Easy to Love Period,* this fortunate couple behave towards' each other in a manner that earns love . . . neither the feeling nor the partner is ever taken for granted. Eventually when the "in love" period wanes, the real love will have become strong and deeply rooted with a life of its own. This second love may not be as sparkling as the first, but neither is it as transient. It can endure forever.

The couple who have this awareness and are willing to work for it will find that when the early vibrancy of their desire begins to decrease, a new sexual attraction will have grown. Not as urgent as the old, perhaps, but richer and more satisfying and capable of lasting all their lives. This, to me, is the secret of "falling in love," marriage and love.

Actually the accepted basis for marriage in this country is so easy, its very simplicity should invoke suspicion. Wear the right clothes, use the right make-up, be popular, be sexy (whatever that means), go out a lot, meet the right guy — fall in love and — Bingo! Marriage!

Marriage is seen not as a vehicle for the deepest joy, or greatest misery, but rather as a means of social and moral justification for sleeping together — to lock in forever the wonderful "in love" state. These are the hopes of millions. Divorcee after divorcee will say: "The next time I marry it will be for love."

"Were you in love with your former husband when you married him?" you ask.

"Well, yes, I guess I was."

"Were you in love with him when you divorced him?"

"No! Of course not!"

"What happened to the love?" A variety of reasons greet this question.

"We were really too young — we were not compatible — he was not Mr. Right."

"He changed after marriage." (Who doesn't?)

"He was selfish," and so on . . .

All the bad marriages, it seems were due to wrongful selection, and now the lesson is learned. Unfortunately, the factors which underwrote the failure of the first marriage will underwrite the dissolution of the next. Nothing is changed, nothing learned. The same adolescent hope prevails — the assurance that something wonderful will come into being without effort.

Our attitude is to treat marriage like a romance and, like romance, which starts effortlessly, marriage is entered into quickly and ends as suddenly. That this is immoral and un-Christian is seldom mentioned from the pulpit. Our culture has woven a web of lies and deceit which cements this unholy state with high but empty phrases. Rather than face the growing disaster, we reinforce the conditions which make it inevitable.

The morality and the attitudes composing our culture are constructed from the building blocks of many previous cultures. We ignore the need to adjust our moral and social code to the vast scientific and technological revolution which has taken place in the last sixty years. Our society, to survive, needs to re-appraise its values if we are to achieve balance and harmony in the face of the glaring contradictions confronting us today.

Each state and religion in its early days tempered its laws and customs to suit the peculiar needs of its time. Greece, with its limited arable land could not support a large population, therefore it considered homosexuality a social norm. In his "Symposium of Love," Plato regarded this type of human relationship as the height of breeding and sophistication in scholars and gentlemen. We, of course, condemn the practice. And, in the harsh Sinai Desert, not very far away, the early Hebrews, fleeing from Pharoah's Egypt, faced with extinction from enemies and an uncertain food supply, clung to life tenaciously. To survive, children were needed to overcome a high mortality rate. The Hebrew Priests issued fearful edicts against homosexuality, birth control, and even masturbation. Excommunication and death faced the violator. "Thou shalt not cast thy seed upon the ground."

These laws were passed not as definitions of right and wrong, virtue and sin, but because geographic and economic conditions and survival demanded such measures.

But rarely did the superior intellect believe that religious laws emanated from God. He knew they were devised for the safety, security and health of the nation. The mass of the population, superstitious and illiterate, could easily be persuaded that such religious injunctions came from God, through his priests.

Today we are torn between our outmoded moral dictums and the physical needs of our bodies. We resolve this conflict by marrying when we "fall in love." Our culture frowns on affairs prior to marriage — so we marry our romance when it is born — and divorce it when it dies. Our bodies and emotions require a continuation of sexual pleasure; we are not content to go on in a sexless monogamous state when the "in love" period with its sexual urgency departs.

In North America we flounder in a no-man's land between the sophisticated aristocrat, who considered lovers and mistresses a vital part of life and the poor peasant who lived in the ever-present fear of hell and damnation on guard against the evils of the flesh. The former had no intention of depriving himself of outside sexual pleasures once he or she was married. The peasant, bowed down by superstition, religion, labor and poverty accepted a sexless monogamous state as a condition for entry into heaven.

Held fast by two powerful forces, we spin around in an endless foredoomed search. Until a few years ago divorce was one avenue of this search; but even this stop-gap reaction to confusion and frustration has not proven to be the answer. We now have more bewildering, artificial aids to fulfillment, all of them disappointing and as disastrous as divorce.

As a means of coping with our unrestructured marital codes, we seek variety in wife-swapping, orgies, pornography and in every type of sexual experiment. Can there be doubt any longer of our confusion, the pressure of our needs, and the contradictory face of society?

Our bodies are sexual, richly endowed by nature to be sensitive, alive and prolific; all nature is caught up in this cycle, to be born, to grow, to mate, to reach a zenith of growth and power, to wane, age and to die. But we do not grow; we are afraid to be sexual; we are ashamed to age and scared to die.

We have little conception of the conditions, training and delineation of objectives needed for a fruitful and happy marriage and we lack the sophistication to sustain love affairs outside marriage. So we blend the two and doom them both. Never was slaughter more cheerfully contracted.

The Eleventh Commandment of divorced mothers to their sons — "Thou shalt have no other woman before me."

Chapter 3

MY MOTHER'S MY PAL

No one can pinpoint the single basic cause of the break-up of a marriage, but one thing *is* clear. Divorce firmly establishes the foundation for future marital discord in the offspring of the divorced.

Each contestant in divorce regards himself as the victim and the other as the principal offender.

There is no doubt we are in the middle of a major evolutionary period where one way of life has gone forever and the new one not yet arrived. Unable to move backward to a lost stability or forward, our generation stumbles blindly along during this transitory period. Since we are unable to see the pattern of society as a whole, we localize our confusion by heaping blame on our spouses.

When trouble arrives in a marriage many mothers sublimate their needs to their children, giving and demanding more love than is normal and healthy. This emotional investment in the children's lives makes them the repository of the mother's hopes and dreams.

A child can never be a substitute for the lost love of a husband. And it is at this point the mother, divorced or partner in a poor marriage, imposes, under the guise of love, a cruel and selfish oppression, the effects of which will endure and torment the child throughout his life.

In her children the mother sows the seeds of everlasting devotion and loyalty. Fresh is the memory of her own broken marriage and, she fears, subconsciously perhaps, that if her husband could leave her so, one day, might her children.

So the stage is set. Using the weapons available to her through age, motherhood and experience, she hourly, daily brainwashes and indoctrinates her children towards life-long servitude to her. Until finally the mother's personality is permanently imprinted on her children. Helplessly they absorb her fears.

This is a most damnable cruelty, this giving and demanding from a child the love normally shared with a husband. Unconsciously the child imbibes the nourishment of future neurosis. As a caged fledgling will not survive if freed too early from the nest, so too will this child, as an adult, be unable to separate and emerge as a whole, integrated person. His avidity for life will be shackled. The guilt and confusion instilled in him in childhood will always be present. Mother will always be there.

Humans, complex creatures though they are, are not so different from other animals and the law of survival demands that the young of the species separate and become an entity embracing by trial and error the rewards and penalties of its own world.

This separation is slowest in the human family. More helpless at birth than any other animal, the baby is surrounded by its mother with food, warmth and love. From conception through gestation, delivery and feeding, mother and child are one. Many women are puzzled and disappointed after the birth of their first child to find that their husband's feelings for the infant are not as intense as their own. This is natural. The husband participated briefly in the experience. With the mother it was an hourly, daily, monthly event. The child was the substance of her very own body.

The child depends totally on its mother. The father remains a shadowy figure until the child takes its first independent step. From then on the father begins to feel a growth of love similar to that the mother experiences. With many mothers, the child's first independent steps are viewed with mixed feelings and a sense of loss.

As the child becomes more independent, there is a corresponding growth of affection in the father as though he had been marking time waiting for this new human to emerge. The pleasure of the father is equally matched by the child's exhilaration as he begins to flex his physical and mental muscles. The child revels in his new freedom and agility. He sees the world as a marvelous playground full of challenge, and whenever he masters a new pinnacle his boundless joy is equally shared by his father. The child sees in his dad an accomplice who participates in his delight.

The child is leaving the womb, the breast and his mother's warm body. Years later, he will rediscover this warmth in another woman. The child is separating, and of all the roles the father plays, the most crucial is to help the child become an independent, complete, human organism. Separation does not mean the child will forget his parents, but rather he moves from a state of dependency to one of self-reliance with a right to taste his own life and to grow.

Such is the development of the young human animal — but precisely the opposite occurs when a mother, disappointed in love and marriage, sublimates her need for a mate in her love for her children. The child remains locked in an emotionally-retarding relationship. Through repression, he adapts to a situation over which he has no control. Years later, this emotional confusion will frustrate and destroy the separate life he will try to build with another woman. Distortions and projected images will haunt him with echoes of the past. His inability to distinguish reality from unresolved, hidden feelings will foster illusion and error. His self image will be shameful and his confidence stunted.

Mother will always be there obscuring his vision. When he looks at his wife he will sometimes see the pure, sexless creature who was his mother and sometimes he'll see a terrible harridan driving him to impotency.

Adding further to the child's dilemma and the man's confusion is a distorted image of his father. He is told that a man is strong and decisive — a woman dependent and submissive. But, at home it is mother who is aggressive, independent and talkative, and father who is passive.

Who does the child follow in this gray area of undetermined sexes? He can't follow his milquetoast father and he dare not — follow his mother — after all, she is a woman — so he steers a confused middle course, neither fish nor fowl. He never develops his God-given right to be a male — aggressive, virile and vigorous.

This then is the future husband and father. This is the Lothario in whom some girl is going to repose her dreams. And this is the guy who falls asleep on the couch after dinner while watching TV. This faded Romeo, this has-been sexpot who prefers TV to his wife's body, is cheating and depriving his wife of her deepest emotional and physical needs.

That he too is a victim will not slow the disintegration of a home where love — physical love — has all but disappeared. Romeo, seemingly, is impotent — at least where his wife is concerned. Another woman will spark him quickly, yet his wife, beside him in bed, will leave him indifferent and fearful that she may make demands on him.

On the odd occasion when his nature overcomes the cords which bind him, his love-making will not be passionate and tender but feelingless and hasty, after which he will turn on his back and go to sleep while his wife, awake in the dark, lies frustrated and miserable.

Women were made for love — tender, ardent love. In love they bloom; without it they shrivel and become nagging shrews. No greater means of achieving unity and harmony can be found between male and female than in love-making. Here, man and woman become one — forsaking all others.

And into this private sanctum steps mother — mother's image — making sure no other woman will ever occupy the place she has built in the heart of her son.

To forestall future competition, unhappy mothers unconsciously convert sons into husbands by proxy. They instill sexual taboos which will insure failure in the future marriage of their sons. Some designing female may get the boy — but not completely. He may get married but the emotional gears won't mesh. Waiting in the wings will be mother.

It's difficult being a feeling human being in our "civilized" society. Basic needs and desires constantly clash with so-called moral standards and ethics. The complexities and interpretations of the words "right" and "wrong" do not bother the very young child but they most certainly surface as he grows older. Everything is clear-cut, black and white — no grays, no variables. The experts in right and wrong are mother, dad, church, school and the state. And they must be right — they are, after all, adults, authorities. But their rightness is one of fearful rigidity and they are more frequently wrong than right. There are a thousand different meanings to the same concept in a thousand different people in different moods, on different occasions.

People en masse have always been fearful and unsure and, as a consequence, leave most of their thinking and decision-making to powerful elites. Laws are promulgated, commandments written, edicts decreed and stages set. Like a fat woman struggling into a too-tight girdle, man groans himself into a preordained image.

A child is born innocent. His functions and motives are simple but strong, few, but instinctive. More than on any other single factor his development hinges on the roles played by his father and mother. Certainly the child does not bring concepts of right and wrong, virtue and sin into the world. Nor is he born with pre-conceived ideas of morality and taboos.

What does the word "love" mean to him? Pliable and highly impressionable, he will pattern his code on that of his parents. In divorce many of mother's values become distorted. Through disappointment and frustration the word "love" metamorphoses into something Madonna-like, spiritual, with all passion erased.

This is not difficult to understand. A "decent" woman reared in our hypocritical, sexually-repressed culture and separated from her natural mate, feels she has to rigidly suppress her normal needs or go to the devil in lust and wantonness. Her religion has told her that virtue is its own reward.

The repression of her natural physical needs takes tremendous effort and the stresses born of inhibition atrophy other well-springs of spontaneous life. Alternatively, should she submit to the needs of her body, she becomes riddled with guilt. There is no middle way. Society and religion have made sure of that.

In this tightly-girded atmosphere the child soon learns to suppress his own feelings. And here his troubles compound, for he now regards his powerful sexual desires as the workings of the devil, dirty and sinful. Every departure from his mother's tormented standards is seen as further proof of his innate weakness and wickedness.

There have always been two sets of standards, two moral codes, one for the rich, and the other for the poor. The rich live above the code, trusting their own private moral concepts and their own needs. The poor place their trust in their religion and the code imposed upon them by their "betters." Without education, refinement and taste, they are only vaguely aware of what they are missing and, in any case, are too poor to do anything about it.

One basis for confusion in America today is that we are the first country in the world to level the erstwhile aristocracy and, at the same time, elevate an illiterate, impoverished peasantry, raising it to standards formerly enjoyed exclusively by the aristocratic rich. This transformation took place over a relatively short period. So short, in fact, that although we now have the tastes and desires of the aristocrat, we fearfully cling to the monogamous, moral code of the illiterate peasant.

Now millions of people only recently freed from the ironclad morality of the peasant class, find themselves in a wealthy, intellectual no-man's land. No longer content with the peasant's simple tastes and sexual inhibitions, *Americans have not as an alternative, developed the aristocratic sophisticated sensual style of life.*

Neither aristocrat nor peasant. So, which standard will the millions follow? Safety lies in an impossible middle course. Maintain the framework of decency, family and religion and, at the same time, express our frustrations in strip-tease houses, massage parlors, orgies and wife-swapping.

The repressed society of America splits gapingly at the seams. And the boy returns to his mother's home with the sad news that his wife has left him. "Don't worry, my darling, you'll always have your mother . . . . "

With a bad girl, money comes first — love later; with a good girl, love first — money later.

Chapter 4

THE DOLLAR COST OF LOVE

In a world where almost all endeavor is measured in terms of money and value received, it is singular that no one measures the dollar value of marriage. In bygone days of chivalry, the reciprocal returns of marriage and the expected rewards to the offspring were shrewdly and carefully assessed by parents. Today, in a most unchivalrous age, this business-like approach has been abandoned. No one calculates the hoped-for returns. At least — men don't. Women and their parents still cling to that old charming custom.

The buying of a horse becomes a sharp practice, attended by shrewd bargaining, careful examination, and rapid appraisal of performance before the purchaser consummates the sale. So it is on most occasions when money is exchanged for goods or services. The subject of money is taboo when love enters the picture, but it is the most eloquent of all when love departs! A cynic once said: "With a bad girl money comes first and love next; with a good girl love first and money later." But rarely does the bad girl try to exact as high a payment as the good girl. Besides, the bad girl has no legal rights, so she can't collect anyway.

Why this subject of money? Let's explore it and see where it takes us. Money represents the crystallized form of a man's productivity and talent. As the sun's energy is stored in the depths of the earth, in the form of coal, so money is man's converted energy, stored as insurance against the time when muscle and productivity wane — so what?

Simply this. The ability to earn money in this highly competitive world is comparable to primitive man's hunting prowess. Since the best hunter was the most popular man in the tribe, modern man competes in the only way left open to him — making money.

No longer able to use bow and arrow, man is conditioned early to hunt for money, and tools are supplied in the form of education and training. Our standards measure a man by his success in hunting money. Under the lash of this ambition he undertakes to work or hunt much harder than he should, subjecting himself to pressure and fatigue that bodies and minds were never built to stand. As a result he frequently achieves retirement and interment at a much earlier age than anticipated. For this contingency, he provides fresh meat for the years ahead in the form of life insurance. He bets he will die early! Man generally accepts the fact that he will work hard all his life. He will not be lazy or a dilettante; society condemns such weakness.

No small feat this. Gone are the romantic dreams of childhood. He goes to work now and television will be his substitute for adventure.

This then, is a man's role in marriage and very relieved are the girl's parents when she "makes a good catch."

Has anyone computed the dollar value of a man's earning power? It's really easy. For example: To earn $8,000 per year on safe stocks, gilt-edged securities, or government bonds, one would have to invest at least $100,000 at eight per cent. Think that over, father of the bride, when the subject dowry is mentioned. To earn $32,000 per year, one would have to invest four times that amount — $400,000 and, to earn $80,000 per year, one would have to invest that wonderful American Dream come true — a million!

All contracts commence with the most common of all legal phrases, *"In consideration of . . ."* implying that in return for what I do, this is what I get. The hunter is a pretty valuable fellow dollar-wise.

Yet, this value, this important contribution to marriage is

made light of and almost forgotten — forgotten, that is, until the wife's attorney starts computing the divorce settlement. And in consideration of this ability to hunt, what does the man expect in return? Why does he marry? Why does he make this girl his partner and beneficiary of the fruits of his hunting? Partner in estate, earnings, insurance and heir to community property and alimony. No need has she, once the ring is slipped on, to punch a time clock or work all day at a job. He will provide. In one fell swoop she has earned security, money, food, clothing and shelter for the rest of her life. And the more successful he is, the larger the cars, the bigger the home, the more expensive the jewelry, the more liberal the pin money, the more extensive the wardrobe, the more numerous the servants, the more colossal the insurance, and the more frequent the vacations.

Why? How does she differ from other women this man continues to meet after he is married, say the waitress in the restaurant, who, if she is especially attentive may get a $2 tip and if she is inefficient, no tip at all; or the secretary in his office who, with 50 other girls, answers an ad, has her references checked, competes in a preliminary test, in order to earn $150 to $200 per week, and who must work and deliver or be fired; or the housekeeper employed at $250 to $350 per month, who, goes through a thorough screening before being selected, and then works anywhere from 8 to 12 hours per day cleaning, cooking, taking care of the kids and attending to the husband's and the wife's needs? What happens to the man's ability to measure value received with one group of women as against another? What happens to the willingness of the waitress, secretary and housekeeper to give a fair return for salary received as employees once they achieve the status of a wife? Why does a man expect so much from one female and so little from the other?

Why therefore marriage, when it produces a redoubling of labor on the man's part and the cessation from work on the part of the wife because she is married?

"In consideration of working for you, providing for you,

supporting you all my life, what will you do for me?''

I would change the marriage ceremony! In spite of the piety of the churches, the vestment of the priests and the music of the choir, the method has not been too successful. I would change the question "Do you take — etc. — to love, honor and obey,'' and replace it with "In consideration of . . . ,'' and spell it out in detail!

In consideration of working for his family all his life, what does the man get in return? What he fails to get is usually the starting point for most of the arguments and bitterness; the precursors to divorce. Men want a woman to give. To give the gifts that only she can bestow, her femininity, her support and her unique ability to make him feel like a man, a hero and a giant. Regardless of whether he is knock-kneed, bald, fat, skinny or hollow-chested. Regardless of whether he earns $100 or $2,000 per week. Unfortunately, these gifts, so easy for a woman to give, are in terribly short supply in this country. The man wants a home, children, meals and affection. It all sounds simple but they are hard to attain. Homes represent responsibility and work to the woman, children spoil her figure, and affection is too valuable a commodity to be given easily.

So the poor slob works harder and harder, thinking if he earns more money, buys a bigger home, a new car, more clothes and jewelry for his wife, he will get a pat on the head. Many men would be grateful for even that but fail to receive it. Why, for heaven sake, does a man expect *so much from a waitress, housekeeper or secretary, for so little paid, and so little from a wife for so much paid?*

Women, I believe, have an instinctive knowledge of the principles of the free enterprise system and a canny awareness of the law of supply and demand. This law decrees that when a commodity is in short supply, the price goes up, since money is more plentiful than the merchandise — but when the commodity is in large supply, the price drops because money now is more valuable than the merchandise. Could it be that many women, determined to confound Nature for not making them men, corner the market of love, affection and wifely functions when they marry? And, since society says that a man may only have one wife and must not cheat, and since all competition has now ceased, wives now artificially shorten the supply of love, affection and service? The frustrated husband works harder in turn, thinking he may achieve more of this precious stuff by making more money, only to create an oversupply of money — making it cheap — whilst the commodity of love, affection and service remain in even shorter supply. Too much affection and love released too soon would ruin the market! If women behaved on dates as they do in marriage, marriage proposals would be few and far between.

Marriages ending in divorce usually follow a familiar pattern. After years of withholding on the part of the wife, doing as little as possible and challenging the man at every turn, the marriage begins to disintegrate. Arguments are the order of the day, trust is replaced by battle lines tightly drawn, and every incident becomes an issue.

Yet, most of the arguments are caused by the husband asking for the bestowal of his wife's unique gifts and the wife stubbornly withholding them.

Quarrels increase, for now the problem is compounded further. Not only is the husband deprived of what he thought he would obtain in marriage, but his very nature is challenged and his ego threatened. He can't hit his wife on the head or kick her in the fanny, a method popular and successful some years ago, but now fallen into disuse and frowned on by the courts. Besides, his mother told him: "Never hit a woman." All he can do is sullenly withdraw, and yell occasionally, or he can cowardly nag and complain, or get drunk or simply walk out. This he rarely does. It's the woman who walks out. I am amazed we aren't a nation of drunks. I am amazed that so many men continue to go home night after night to the endless battles, frustrations and withholding, instead of setting up a mistress, where, with less cash and energy, these rare commodities of love and admiration and perhaps even a meal cooked with love, lit with candles and blessed with wine, would be gladly given by a woman not yet become a wife.

In our society, Nature, with her law of compensation has supplied excellent alternatives to replace the vacuums that exist in so many homes. The functions that a man seeks in a wife can be easily supplied by other sources. Despite the artificial premium women have foolishly imposed, love, affection and homemaking are not really in short supply.

Good meals can be obtained in a variety of restaurants and, for an extra dollar — not a new Chevrolet — the waitress will fuss and cluck and attend your needs as though you were a Crown Prince! Apartments of all shapes, sizes, furnished and unfurnished, are there for the asking. Laundries and cleaners will compete for work — even come to the door. Restaurants will deliver food, friends are to be had by the hundreds — the only rules are, each must give of themselves. And as for women, once more the law of supply and demand is restored, and the man becomes the sought-after creature. Dates are on their best behavior, each vies with the other to make the man the King. Woe betide the date who withholds herself, demanding gifts and giving nothing in return or who argues and sets up challenges to show the man how much smarter she is! The woods are thick with females, single, divorced — thousands of them — all anxious to please. Oh, how nice and well-behaved they are — attractively groomed and excessively feminine.

The company of men on occasion is stimulating. There are trips and discoveries to be made and Tahiti is not that far away. In eleven hours one can be in Paris or London. So Nature adjusts the deficits in marriage by making plentiful the commodities of love and affection at the end of marriage. While, during marriage, the "poor relation," the husband, continues to starve.

Is this mercenary, this measuring of affection and admiration in terms of money? Many marriages are a process of "gimmee, gimmee" things that money will buy; and the unmercenary attitude of a woman in the divorce courts is a sight to behold!

It would seem, therefore, that the dollar value of love strikes a normal balance in the competitive society of the single state, but in marriage, man's greatest offering, his ability to make a living, is reduced to nothing, and, as nothing, requires nothing of a woman in return!

Sad as it is, the world has turned around, the sexes reversed. Just a few years ago it was women who worked their backs off in marriage, raising four, six, ten or twelve kids, cooking, cleaning, loving, nursing and sacrificing everything to make a successful marriage, in spite of some husbands who chose not to work, stayed out late, drank too much and contributed little to the marriage.

Today, it's the husband who comes home early and the wife who stays out late. It's the husband who wants to be married and the wife who seeks the divorce. It's the husband who breaks his back at work and frequently at home, while the wife spends most of her time figuring out how to evade work in the home and spend more time outside on her own amusement. Sad world.

Today women have achieved freedom — freedom to work outside the home, freedom to compete with men, freedom from marriage — and freedom to be alone.

Chapter 5

THE (GRAY) DIVORCEE

The end of a marriage is like a little death, but to some married women, freedom looks like life after death. Young again, no one to tell her what to do, no more demands, criticisms. No more dinners to cook — no slavery! And, just outside, bright lights, gay conversation, lighthearted friends, flirtations and adventures. Palm Springs, Vegas, here I come! A free spirit again! Oh, what a wonderful world it will be. No more arguments, complaints, no more asking for money. I'll have my own for ever more! Do you know a good attorney?

As these thoughts flit through the mind of our potential divorcee, thoughts of another color harass the husband when visions of a marital split loom. Loneliness, dejection, life in a bleak room, no family, roots or meaning to work and life. These visions are, of course, totally unreal; reality, in fact, is completely the reverse. For, while the woman rushes headlong towards freedom, it is the grim prospect conjured up by the husband which awaits her arrival. And while the husband dreads divorce, the future awaiting him is the rosy prospect envisioned by his wife.

The man's world changes drastically in marriage. For thousands of years his supremacy had gone unchallenged — until the first quarter of this century. And, while most men would swear that women are wrecking the ancient pattern, nothing could be further from the truth. Certainly, women are knocking at the door and yelling for admittance, and men will testify they have taken over. But, they haven't really. They are unsuccessfully trying to fill a vacuum created when men gave up without a struggle.

The male dreads divorce, yet is powerless to avert it. His mental muscles grow weaker as his confidence shrinks; the prospects of divorce are frightening. What will he — poor, helpless victim — do? Lonely, despised, rejected, what will he do after a day's work? Where will he go weekends? He paints a gloomy picture. And, conversely, the wife, who had been developing self assurance as head of the house, sees divorce as the road to freedom. She's capable and confident. She'll have money, dates, men and above all, she will live! Open the door!

If only they both knew what was about to happen. How confident and calm the man would be. And how cautious the wife. Outside, it is not a woman's world at all! It is still a man's world, firmly established with lines tightly drawn and jealously guarded.

Most disillusioning of all is the fact that members of her own sex, spinsters and divorcees who have gone before, are doing their utmost not only to survive in a man's world, but helping, with every feminine art and allure, to sustain male sovereignty.

Did you know this, Ms. Divorcee? This surely is the bitterest of all pills. You have now joined the ranks of the divorced, and will strive as you never did in marriage to keep intact the male world.

The husband, on the other hand, whom Mommy doesn't love any more, makes the scene with uncertainty. His ego is crushed — he lost the only girl in the world who would love him. Then he rubs his eyes, pinches himself. It can't be true, he says. Where has he been all these years? For he, too, finds it is still a man's world. And be he fat, short, bald, skinny or broke, there are hordes of available women, all on their best behavior, never challenging him and always attentive and flattering.

His ego soars and, as his self-esteem grows, his repressed personality flowers and, for the first time in years he says: "God, I feel alive!"

And what of our new divorcee? The family home is large and strangely quiet, and, although she has the children, they seem to get on her nerves more frequently. They exacerbate the situation, for they now seem to have the idea, in the absence of daddy, that it's a children's world!

For the first few months, things do seem to improve. The cessation of hostilities is pleasant. Since the wife, for years, experienced an emotional tug-of-war in her mixed-up role as woman, wife and leader, the sudden severance brings temporary relief. But only temporary.

What is the chief preoccupation of our newly arrived divorcee? Career, children, home, travel, art, politics, friends. No, it's men! Where do these men come from? What are they like? What do they want? What have they been doing?

Hope is wonderful, but fantasy can be catastrophic! Many women, divorced or married and contemplating divorce, are sure that somewhere outside there is a man who will have all the virtues of her husband and none of his vices. From this starting point, divorcees start the great search.

It is obvious that the husband must have had some good points — hence the original marriage. The fact the husband is a known quantity and the new man an unknown hazard, places him far ahead of the stranger. There is a good chance that another man may have similar or even more pronounced defects, since he lives in the same culture with the same standards and values. Further, how can our gal judge clearly? How does she know she won't repeat the same mistake?

Her problem is further compounded. In her first marriage, she was trusting and open — now she is certain to be more cynical and guarded.

In the selection of a new mate, she must take into consideration the fact he may not want someone else's youngsters — can she be sure he will be good to them? And if indeed the new man is kind, there is always the chance the children may imperil their marital bliss by serving as a constant reminder they are not his own.

Where does this dream man come from?

Divorcees are usually between the ages of twenty-eight and thirty-nine at starting point. Some actually get older each year

— many women prefer men a little older than themselves although mature women often prefer younger companions, but conversely, most men prefer younger women. There are more women 18 to 25 years of age, who prefer 35-45 year-old men than there are 18-25 year-old men chasing 35-45 year old women.

There are basically two categories of men in this age group, the divorced and the never married. Our gal tries to avoid the latter. He spells trouble — a mother or a mother's memory lurking somewhere in the background. He's probably set in his ways, old-womanish or a happy seducer with a hell of a history. Or — he's just not moved by women. In any event, the outlook is far from kosher. That leaves the man who has been married. Why did his wife divorce him? He might be as poor a bet as one's ex-husband. You would have to live out of wedlock with him for years before you found out, but you could lose the kids that way.

Well, the field is narrowed to ages 35-40. We'll take a chance that he has been married before. What should he look like? Well, as long as we're changing husbands, he certainly should be good-looking. Tall? Sure! Virile? Of course! Didn't we say that one of the troubles with our husbands was their indifference to sex? Actually, he should be a little like Cary Grant, have a nice speaking voice, be a good conversationalist, popular with men, romantic, decisive, tender, poetic, passionate, and above all, understanding. And he shouldn't have a mother!

He should have unlimited money and an interesting career — not a blouse manufacturer, or an auctioneer — a writer perhaps, or a lecturer, diplomat, or maybe just a millionaire. "After all, I want my kids to have the best. Why make a change if I don't improve myself? And he should love me completely and never make demands on me or be possessive. Nor should he ever criticize my housekeeping. He should never be tired, preoccupied or make an issue about money. He should take me away weekends, and out to a nice restaurant on Sunday morning for breakfast. We would travel a lot, and he should always be interested, completely interested in me!''

There are several million women, married, single and divorced looking for this hero — and he hasn't been found yet. But the girls keep hoping and looking.

The only place he exists is in a hit record, on a TV or movie screen or in one's imagination.

Forget the dreams of money, charm, career, manliness and decisiveness — and the chances of landing a skinny, broke thin-haired, petulant, hollow-chested male are great.

The male has suddenly become King! All the gals are after him. His stock has leaped upwards; he never had it so good, and, he's going to keep it coming. Marriage? Hell, that would end it all! He doesn't have to do anything. He's a male.

The chances of landing the ideal man is one in a million. Have you ever considered, ladies, the attitude of the eligible male? Marriage is the last thing he wants! Suddenly, the world has become his oyster and, after years of marriage, monotony and misery, his ego crushed, his manhood challenged, he's free and it's a man's world. Daily, he is reminded by suppliant females that he's a hero! Why should he give that up! Besides, he's wily and experienced; he has learned the hard way.

He isn't going to be trapped by promises of home-cooked meals, a seductive figure and the prospect of heady nights beside the TV. Like an old salmon in a well-fished stream, he can smell the hook a mile away.

The ex-husband knows this moment of triumph all too quickly comes to an end once he says: "I do," He knows the law is slanted towards the female, and he knows there are thousands of attorneys all ready to aid the "little woman" once she decides to shed her husband and enjoy his substance. Why should he fall for that?

What does he want? It's really very simple. An occasional date, proper respect and then to bed — no strings. And when he takes you to bed he feels he's doing you a service! Oh, he's a hard man. Of course you don't have to go to bed with him. If he really digs you, he might wait three, maybe four dates, and then, no bed and he's gone. So you do go to bed; after all, you're human and he's likeable. From the moment of conquest he starts a rear guard action. Demonstrations of affection from you are regarded as warning signals, and he starts to pull away.

And so, life passes pleasantly for our male. He has his work, friends, apartment, vacations, ball games, and of course, his women, all loving, never demanding, never possessive, and all telling him what a wonderful lover he is. And then there are so many women out there he hasn't yet met. What an exciting prospect!

But you say, "He's a fool. He doesn't know what he's missing — a home, a family, a loving wife, permanence, security, building something together." But, he does know what he's missing. He had a home — worked hard to get it. His wife got that! He had a family, and loved his kids. His wife got those too. Permanence he never had — his wife's attorney shattered his hearth. Security, — here today, gone tomorrow. The things he built with his wife, his wife and her attorney shared between them. Ms. Divorcee, you have paved the way for another woman's failure to catch a man, and another woman has facilitated your failure.

Men complain about unfair divorce laws, the flimsy excuses women use to obtain divorces, the distribution of the hard-worked-for assets, the alimony, and they say, it's all one-sided. Like hell it is! Your wife picks up the tab with your money when she takes her boy-friend out to dinner? And then some other husband pays the tab when his ex-wife takes you out. Things balance out.

To meet this shift in social standards and provide a place where lonely women might meet men, some bright girls started a club which has enjoyed some success. It's called "Parents Without Spouses." Because there are so few places where divorcees can meet men, "Parents Without Spouses" sponsors dances. Divorcees eagerly anticipate these events, dress carefully, and sally forth to the big adventure.

I have never seen the Chicago stock yards — but I have seen

these dances! They are frightening and desperate like a slave auction! The allure of the female fades as hordes of them smile, gesture, pose and parade. Strong men blanch and retreat to the security of quiet bars. The market is reversed and the man is desperately hunted, but he doesn't want to be chased — he wants to do the chasing! There is something frightening about being chased by a female and being chased by a thousand is positively terrifying.

There was once a movie called the "The Gay Divorcee." A charming, beautiful, divorced woman was depicted floating from one deliriously exciting adventure to another. Admired, flattered by an army of doting males, envied by her poor married sisters, she became a sort of symbol for American womanhood. The longed for, hoped for state of freedom. But this was a movie, it was fiction and fantasy, yet our Cinderella mentality still continues.

Most divorcees sit at home at night and when the phone rings it is a reprieve. Parents are really no help, they only remind you you're getting older and lonelier.

Married friends feel a little uncomfortable with you, on guard lest you think them patronizing. They eventually disappear. You got the kids, and you got the responsibilities. Double. Other divorced women speak your language but you hate it! On vacations word gets around that you're a divorcee and immediately ideas are formed about you. Married women think you are loose and dangerous — and cluck protectively around their husbands. Men are amazed if you don't jump in the hay with them after the first drink. You've lost your citizenship, your status! You have freedom — you stay home. Night after night as the hours tick away, loneliness is increased by fear. Self-confidence begins to ooze away, and in that quiet apartment a ghost enters and takes you by the hand. You wonder if you've forgotten how to talk, how to be witty. You begin to feel unattractive, despised.

Given enough time in that room, and whatever ugly mental self-image you have concealed all these years, gradually emerges and takes over. So you rush out (if you can get a sitter) to the nearest bar, the nearest friend or to "Parents Without Spouses." Or you get on the telephone and start calling. Striving to keep a cheerful note in your voice, and having nothing new to say, you ask, "What's new?" When women friends' numbers give out, you have a slug of Scotch and apprehensively dial some men friends, hoping they are not entertaining other females. Trying to sound casual, and praying your anxiety won't show, you chattily ask: "What's new? I haven't heard from you for some time. Been out of town? Yes, we must get together sometime." Maybe I should have gone to bed with him last time — he sounded a little cold.

A date brings relief, but the loneliness of yesterday is the herald of tomorrow's fears.

Millions of women know this. Yet today there are thousands of women about to tell their husbands they have decided to get a divorce, and tomorrow there will be thousands more.

When birth control became generally accepted, intelligent women quickly availed themselves of this simple technique. The need warranted the use. Is there not as great a need for divorce control? Why is one precaution so important, the other non-existent?

The entire national advertising campaign is aimed at her Majesty. She is flattered, cajoled and wheedled. Each woman is personally appealed to by manufacturers who feign great respect for her opinions. Her ego is boosted while her purse strings are loosened.

Chapter 6

THE AMERICAN WOMAN

Much has been written about the American woman. Yet little light has been shed upon this baffling creature whose mysterious wants are so perplexing to the male, and whose unique feelings he so often misinterprets in terms of his own needs. The concept of the American woman runs all the way from the apron-clad homebody of the TV commercial to the voluptuous sex-pot of the girlie magazines. She is extolled as a paragon of the 20th century in her role of wife, mother, lover, mechanic, club woman and friend.

But for every exaggerated "pro," we can find an equally inflated "con." Her sex is compared to the ocean with its calms and sudden squalls; she is associated with the moon, placid and cool, the earth bears her name, and ships her gender. Sometimes it is hard to know whether the male is the father of the child or the female — the mother of the man.

The female was an important deity in pre-Christian religions. Isis ruled with Osiris in Egypt, Athena and Aphrodite battled in Greece and Troy. Venus was deified by Rome and has been worshipped ever since. Mona Lisa sums them all up — mysterious, magnetic and all-knowing.

But until the turn of this century, in many countries, women were treated, (so we think) as second-class citizens, and sometimes as possessed of the devil — unclean. Men have always feared them; witness the measures they invoked in some cultures to isolate them, keep them indoors, screen their faces and deny them rights that men enjoyed.

All this has changed in a few short years — for the better it seems. But, along with this change, has come the vast social illness of divorce and broken homes.

Yet, prior to the turn of this century, we did not live in barbarism. Religions flourished, great liberators and thinkers were born, taught and improved life, Christ walked, the Magna Carta was signed, wars of freedom were won, and still, women were considered inferior. But few great minds did anything to emancipate women who remained in pretty much the same status until the early 20th century.

Could it be the guardians of the status quo in their wisdom envisaged a condition as ridiculous as that which exists today whenever the concept of FEMININE FREEDOM crossed their minds?

Did all these great historical liberators forget women's rights? Did they concentrate so hard on man's inhumanity to man that they overlooked man's inhumanity to woman? Or did they know something we have forgotten — that a woman, to be fulfilled, must satisfy her own basic need by being truly a woman. Not a swordsman, hunter, plowman, artisan or statesman — but a woman. And that the less she follows male pursuits, the more she realizes her own destiny.

In 60 short years, all this has been reversed. Today, women have achieved "SUCCESS" with a bang, in what was considered man's exclusive domain — and they are hammering down the few remaining doors.

So a great victory is won. Fears of weakness and inadequacy are dispelled. And women tell themselves that after thousands of years of subjugation, they have finally proved they are as good as men and entitled to respect, rewards and the right to be treated as one of the guys. To be treated — as a man!

But there is a precept that holds that for every gain made there is a corresponding loss. For if, indeed, the gains made by women are valid and women have grown stronger, more independent and capable, then it is also true that men have grown correspondingly weaker, more dependent and less assertive, as so many married women sadly discover.

And marriages have become more short-lived, perplexing, and loveless. As a people we have become more lonely and neurotic and our children more bewildered and insecure. Marriage has become a joke and, as often as you hear of a new marriage, you hear of a corresponding divorce. Much is said in print and from the pulpit deploring modern social conditions but few dare to attack the root of the illness. So, the sickness continues.

Women have won the race and lost the prize, like children who have outrun their fathers and who are bewildered by their dads' diminished statures.

Women complain today about the growing softness and femininity in men, their lack of ardor in lovemaking and their inability to treat women as females. Where there is a vacuum nature steps in and, in millions of families, the wife is forced into the decision making role. With a dominant wife, the male retreats and thereby earns his wife's contempt and an acceleration of her aggressiveness. She atrophies her femininity by making more and more decisions, while her husband drifts further away from responsibility.

The irony and the sadness of it! To try so hard for equality with men and to lose so much in its achievement.

If wealth and possessions were measures of happiness we surely would be the happiest nation the world has known. But we are not; we defer all to money making, and unfortunately for men and women who might one day have come to their senses, business is quick to exploit this flaw in American life. Recognizing the dominant position of the wife in the home, the entire national merchandising campaign is aimed at Her Majesty. She is flattered, cajoled and wheedled; each woman is personally appealed to by manufacturers who feign great respect for her opinion. Since she makes most of the decisions on cars, vacations, homes, furnishings and clothing, her ego is boosted while her purse-strings are loosened.

The dealer knows the husband is not so vulnerable to an emotional appeal, not so frequently an impulse buyer. Men will go on using an item of merchandise long after Madison Avenue has declared it passe.

With business bowing to greed and the entertainment industries avoiding controversy because sponsors are quick to crack down on non-conformity, predigested pap is continually fed into the mind of the nation. Lawmakers count votes rather than the public good and the image makers strive to turn us into a nation of cardboard people. Madison Avenue reaches into every home (subliminal perception is at hand), and bombards children every day with hard-selling dollar-hungry T.V. commercials. In this mad drive that equates consumerism with happiness, what chance does the individual have of developing a healthy appraisal of morality and good taste?

Swept in this maelstrom of money-making, we shrug and mutter, "What can we do about it?" There are more pressing problems such as making the car and house payments and our everlasting concern over business and profits.

Improvement in conditions, industrial, political or social, can come only with the enormous concerted effort of many people. Today there is no movement afoot to cure our national number one epidemic — divorce.

Implanted in all our minds, starting with the young, is the illusion that we can enjoy all the freedoms and combine them with a marriage which will include love, home, passion, children and the endless acquisition of possessions.

Like automatons, we rush blindly into matrimony with no fear of the shadow which hangs over the ceremony — that a scant six percent may find happiness and a good seventy percent will end in divorce. But on we plunge, armed with nothing but "that certain feeling" and high hopes.

To understand the American woman we have to understand the American male — if we can! Is he different from his South American and European counterparts? He certainly is! He has more wealth, can rise faster and go further than other people in any part of the world. If this is the criterion for successful living then he is most successful.

He sees economic prosperity as the only objective so he hitches his wagon to that bewildering star. It promises admiration, status and love, but delivers none. The male drives on to more desperate efforts before the inevitable heart attack sets in. Why does he do this, foresaking all else? Why is the Golden Calf the focus of all ambition so that his sense of values is diminished? Awareness is stifled by an unwillingness to read, or reason and, perhaps take an unpopular position and follow it to the end. Instead he swallows the preconceived opinions of commentators and columnists crediting these pundits with an omnipotence far beyond their wisdom or worth.

Sometimes it is hard to believe that the omniscience of a Cronkite or a Reston was never earned at the ballot box or bestowed by holy oil.

These columnists have been doing it for so long that a visitor to these shores might well marvel, not only at their impertinence, but at their style which makes no concession to humility. Occasionally, some daring soul dares make a disparaging observation whereupon Their Imperial Presences, sheltered behind TV, radio and hundreds of newspapers, quickly rend the heretic.

This willingness to leave opinions and doubts to others in order to focus all one's energy on money making has serious consequences. Over the years it weakens and destroys the individual's powers of independent thought, and as a result it strengthens the image-makers through the public's increasing dependence upon them.

What has all this to do with the American male? Just this: In order to devote all his time and talents to "getting on" the American male narrows his horizons and neglects to evaluate his life and real needs. It never occurs to him that he is throwing away the best part of his life in a pursuit that will never make him and his family happy.

Another constituent must be added to the male disorientation with life. The American male has two powerful ancestors who still shadow and influence him — the Pilgrim Fathers and the millions of European immigrants who followed. The Pilgrims went through misery in Europe to gain freedom of worship, and then on finding it in America, passed along the misery to anyone not of their own persuasion. As a major tenet of their Godliness, the Puritans viewed the five senses with something approaching horror and shame — touch, sight, smell, taste and hearing — the gauges which determine the intensity of living.

The Puritans set to work to remove the threat of sensual pleasure but, unfortunately, the reduction of sensual feeling is the reduction of life itself. The word sensuality to the Pilgrims (and still to us) had a wicked ring. Actually, it is God-given, for if life is given by God then the richer the senses, the richer the life.

To our forefathers this was the work of the Devil. They wore drab clothes, walked with serious miens, shunned laughter as the clarions of indolence and sensuality and sang psalms. Touching, feeling, love, warmth, tenderness and passion were to be avoided. Life was serious and sex was necessary only for procreation. Somehow God had slipped up there. They would have devised other means of perpetuating the race and the herds, but if you have to procreate then you should do so without pleasure.

God made man in His own image with a need for love and human warmth. The Puritans put man in cold storage.

The early work was well done and today we see the struggle taking place in Americans — more in men, it seems than women. Desperately they try to emerge from the ice-box, yet they seal the lid more tightly with restrictions and inhibitions.

Our second ancestor was not quite so subtle, nor did he presume to interpret the Word of God as did the Puritan.

In millions he came to make his way in the new land. His motherland offered him no opportunity — only a perpetuation of the humble pattern of life followed by his lowly forefathers. From peasant stock and working people, they were blind followers of a morality scorned by the aristocracy in their own land.

America gave him the opportunity to "get on," to rise to unimagined heights. This was the promised land. After centuries of merely existing, everything now was possible. Adapting to the pattern set by earlier immigrants who now had amassed homes, flocks, and other possessions, the new citizens became ready disciples of the work ethic.

He was no sensualist. Gratification of the senses was for sometime in the future after "he had got his." Unfortunately, this never happened. The pattern of work blotted out all else and, after the first ambition was achieved, another took its place. Work became an end in itself and its own justification.

From an aristocracy beyond reach to a capitalist status within grasp, he rolled up his sleeves and made work his gospel. Since there are many degrees of financial success, there is no place in the pursuit of the American Dream to stop and gather the family to one's bosom, check one's sensual pulse and start living. Rather, it is a race against time. There always is a larger house, a larger company and a bigger slice of the pie. Financial success always becomes equated with warmth and love.

Wine is sensual, bourbon is sodden; music is sensual, we deaden our perceptions with cacophony; food can be sensual when cooked with love — and we gulp down huge steaks. Smells are sensual, plastic flowers are durable; sight is sensual and we blind ourselves with television and billboards; touch is sensual but time is money so, we make love in a hurry. And if there is one ingredient needed in sensuality it is time, leisure and a wanton, indolent, indifference to the clock.

This then is the heritage of the American male, who is now cast in the role as husband, father and lover.

Nature will not be cheated. She has her own program of right and wrong and, having successfully patterned the world for millions of years, she will not now be thwarted in her design. In our pathetic attempts to mold men and women into unnatural designs we are cracking society wide open.

In our acceptance of the Puritan ethic and the images created by motion pictures and TV we create an anomalous picture of men and women being great lovers and marital partners, when in truth they are poor lovers and ill-equipped candidates for marriage.

In the blind fervor of amassing money we encourage the very elements which destroy the male-female relationship.

These are the basic ends which shape the behavior of many men in this country. The perpetuation of the clannishness and callowness of boyhood is exemplified by the American male's devotion to "good, clean sport" such as baseball and football, his utter loyalty to his all-male club or lodge, his terrible concern for masculinity, his never-to-be-forgotten alma mater, his contempt for eggheads, and suspicion of intellectuals. These, and his dismissal of tenderness, and courtesy as "a bunch of crap" stamp him as a *regular fellow* and the despair of women.

When the media-induced notions of love and marriage have begun to wear thin, the American wife, faced with reality, begins to discover that love, passion and tenderness, those things she wants most in a man, are in short supply. Ignoring the reasons behind this cultural conditioning she steadfastly maintains her dream and says: "I married the wrong guy."

Making little effort to bring out the submerged possibilities in her spouse, she compounds the condition which brought her mate to this unhappy state. Keeping a tight rein on her feelings, she denies her man the real pleasure of her essential nature. Contact is maintained by adventures on safely-trodden paths, movies, radio, TV and drinking.

Denying her natural inclinations as a female, she views her own warmth and need for contact with distrust. She turns her back on her own intuitive femininity and subscribes instead to a shallow concept of what is proposed by hard-sell commercialism. One wonders if she makes such mistakes innocently, a victim of advertising, or does she fear the disclosure of real feelings? In any event she dons the protective mask worn by millions of her sisters.

Every woman is born with all the basic qualities needed to attract the male; her essence, her nature and her uniqueness. Sadly the female ignores her own uniqueness in a frantic attempt to be a poor imitation of some popular celebrity held out at that moment, by the media as the quintessence of womanhood. Deliberately she grinds her own personality into the dust and evolves into a poor imitation of the figure she is currently copying. Never was the poverty of artificiality more evident than here. At best we have a poor facsimile of the original and, at worse, the obliteration of her own nature. Who does the man clutch to his bosom when he moves in, Bardot, Lollibrigida, Marilyn Monroe or Jackie Kennedy? If any of these women are admired, the admiration stems from their own individuality.

The exciting truth, that man can find in every woman a new, exciting mystery, evades the thinking of millions of women in their never-ending quest not to be themselves but a mass-produced, second best. Instead of being just herself to the male, she brings a copy of someone else. Charm, allure and excitement were never purchased in a bottle, tube or wrapper.

Apart from the many basic characteristics which contribute to the charm of women, there are several which appeal to men of all ages. And strangely enough, although they come for free, they are ignored by nearly all American women.

HAIR— WALK — VOICE — FEMININE RETICENCE. Four simple fundamental female qualities. Long, well-brushed, clean hair is one of the loveliest adornments in a woman. There is hardly a man whose head won't turn at the sight of a female with tumbling, long hair. Yet women so often cut their hair short. Where is the profit? What is the reason? Because everyone else does it? Samson's hair was shorn and he became weak. Women's hair was cut and she became strong — better they both had kept their hair.

In few Western countries do women walk gracefully. Without high fashion and labor-saving devices, native women in poorer countries are naturally lithe and harmonious in movement. The sight of a girl in Bali, Ceylon or Tahiti gracefully walking while balancing a heavy package on her head is enough to make the Westerner whistle with appreciation.

For some reason the opinion exists that the female cannot be "sexy" unless the quality is purchased for money. Consequently, greater and more lasting possibilities of feminine attractiveness are ignored. The female body is a lyrical composition of bone, muscles and sinews, blended in a flowing harmony. This mystery has charmed and perplexed artists for thousands of years and the single circumstance when all this beauty comes into play is in the walk. And conversely, this beauty can be dismissed as a travesty when the walk becomes a hobble. American women seem to be indifferent to the potential allure they throw away.

Why do women reject this asset? It is feminine; it does attract men. Is it possible that women are ignorant of their femininity or that deep down they do not want to be feminine? Women hobble, paddle, lunge, stride, and amble as though their legs were burdensome. Many appear to defy the very anatomical design of their bodies. Some walk as though in apology, as though they hated the effort.

Another toll levied on American womanhood by modern life is the almost total neglect of the value and potential of the voice. The term "American accent" is a misnomer. Rarely does climate, geography, or education influence an American accent. Rather, it stems from laziness and an ignorance of the lovely sounds that can emanate from the human larynx.

The human voice can be the loveliest sound in nature. The English language, blended and enriched over hundreds of years, distilling itself ever upwards, gives pleasure whenever it is spoken by an educated English woman. English is the language of literature and poetry, from Chaucer to Shakespeare, from Milton to Churchill. It is a gift to all men, women and children in this country. Yet, the music, timbre and quality, and sound of the language are daily torn to shreds.

In the beginning was the WORD. Actually it is second in human contact, the eyes meet first and commune. Then, what shock and disappointment, when a lovely mouth opens and out comes an ugly sound. How little is it appreciated that the voice is one of the greatest of all sexual attractions. A thousand nuances and colors are possible. It is the sound of desire, of warmth, of humanity.

There are few women who have not at some time thrilled to the sound of an exciting man's voice. Yet few have tried to practice this art. Many men have reacted to the sound of a husky, promising female voice. Yet few men have tried to acquire this asset. Singers have to practice to make a lovely sound — it doesn't come with birth.

FEMININE RETICENCE: This last ingredient of feminine allure is perhaps the most subtle and difficult of all to describe. How do you put into words, the very essence of a woman? Without this, lovely hair, a pleasing voice and a graceful walk will carry the female only part way toward her goal.

Would it be over-simplifying to suggest that the lamentable absence of reticence in many women arises from the conviction they have been cheated by being born female?

Historians tell us that women have occupied a secondary place in society since the beginning of history. But, maybe they are wrong. Maybe women did not occupy a secondary place, but a primary place — primary as women that is. Certainly, for thousands of years, women were more fulfilled in the role of wife, mother and mistress, than they are today. It would be interesting to list the deprivations sustained by women up to the time of the suffragettes and compare these wrongs to the unhappiness experienced by so many women today in broken marriages and wrecked homes. I wonder what Mrs. Pankhurst would say if she saw the suffering of women in their hopeless quest for love through the "total freedom" they have now achieved in divorce.

The day Mrs. Pankhurst and her female supporters chained themselves to the gates of Buckingham Palace, a battle was begun — and, femininity was lost.

For thousands of years nature has evolved. Bees did not envy horses, horses had no wish to be elephants, and an elephant wouldn't give you a thank you for the privilege of being a snake. The sun did not envy the moon and each star pursued its prescribed course. In people too, there were differences. There were philosophers, hermits, prophets, soldiers and saints. And even though a soldier would occasionally become a saint, and a saint a soldier, one's role was best achieved by the fitting of the work, to the personality, strength, talent and type of each individual.

The suffragettes, in one swoop, changed all that and made women feel they were the downtrodden, forgotten race. They made women ashamed of their role. What Mrs. Pankhurst did not anticipate was that a mass-produced society would harness itself to this new feminine freedom and send it rolling along at a thousand miles per hour gathering momentum and burning up everything in its path.

Today, women have achieved freedom — freedom to work outside the home, freedom to compete with men, freedom from marriage and freedom to be alone and confused.

I believe that the Pankhurst suffragette movement, the machine age, two world wars, and the advancement of mass production, spelled the end of femininity and replaced it with a lacquered veneer. I don't believe Mrs. Pankhurst intended her movement to become the vanguard of today's women's lib movement. What set out to be a campaign for the redressment of a few inequities ended in a war to end women's role entirely. Tragically it is a war without end. Were the women's liberation movement to achieve all the goals it seeks today, tomorrow there would be a new compilation of grievances. This revolution is a war that can never be won for conquest spells failure.

Unable to stop at the original goals, emancipation presses ever onwards, trampling all that was good and desirable in women's nature.

You can't be a captain of industry in charge of hundreds of employees, and remain feminine. You can't climb the ladder of business and commerce without having the gentle curves angularized and then knocked off. You can't win in competition with man and remain demure and submissive. You have to push harder than your male competitor in this unnatural element.

So the fearful cycle grinds ever onward — the female demands equality so that she may remain independent. Then she

gets married — then divorced. And now the career she demanded before marriage, and for which she prepared herself,
comes to her rescue. She was never trained for marriage — her
early training prepared her for single security *after* marriage. If
women were not trained to earn a living the loss of such talent
would be felt less in marriage and marriage might become more
rewarding and lasting. Certainly pre-marital training in weapons
and logistics are no help at a peace conference except to
potential hostile belligerents.

The eternal female. All men dream about her. Who is she?
Where can she be found? Like a lovely, mysterious isle that
emerges suddenly from the depths of the South Seas, and then
— vanishes. Most men never find her, except to dream in an
awakened youthful moment. Some men never give up the
search. Strange, but even though most men never see her, all
men would recognize her.

Is it her eyelashes in a box, her Revlon nail polish, her
foundation cream, the dye in her hair, her Maidenform bra, or
any of the substitutes that pass for feminine allure? Who is she?
It is woman herself! Glorious, honest and self-avowed female.
Glad to be female. Glad to be the opposite of the male.
Rejoicing in the fact that she is not as strong as the male or as
capable in male pursuits — but no stranger in her female
domain. She doesn't feel nature dealt her a cruel blow in
making her the "weaker sex." Like the wind in the trees she is
as free as the air. All the elements are combined in her — earth,
water, fire and air. Compared to this divine creature, man is a
poor, drab animal — but where do you find her? In Hollywood?

She is reticent. She has no need to argue or shove, she
doesn't want to compete with men. She has the quiet satisfaction of knowing that men will compete for her! She has no
desire to play fullback — she can win more games with her
gossamer lures. Intuitively, she knows the strength of her
femininity and has no need to diminish the male; why should
she when she needs him as a counterpart for her femininity? She
does not wish to emulate him, for then she would be half male
and half female. The more male he is, the more pleasure and

delight there is in her femaleness. She does not seek to emasculate him bit by bit, for what profit is there in a eunuch lover?

Witness the tragic reversal of all this — women trying to be like men, and men backing down all the way. The never-ending ambition to show the husband what a nice but stupid chump he is. The female know-it-all. In the relationship today between men and women it is more like two people of the same sex living together.

Surely women dream of becoming this type of female. Why then is it that a man may search an entire lifetime and never find that rare female Shakespeare had in mind when he said, "Age cannot wither her style, nor custom stale her infinite variety."

The Penis, faced with the female's challenge and masculinity, shrinks and recoils; but rises forth proudly and gallantly in response to the soft, gentle female whom nature had in mind for this tribute.

Chapter 7

LOVE WITHOUT SEX —
SEX WITHOUT LOVE

Traditions and laws regulating sexual behavior have changed many times in different countries and eras. There are endless variations on this theme, ranging all the way from the incestuous brother-sister relationship of Isis and Osiris of ancient Egypt to the homosexuality expressed in Plato's "Symposium of Love," from the worldly Roman enjoyment of sex to the chastity of the early Christian mystics.

The pressing needs of sex, its indulgence or its prohibition, have played an enormous role in peoples' lives and in their laws and religion. Temples have been dedicated to celibates and, at other times, to procurers and priestesses of love.

No custom prevails forever. No one law is the absolute of God and man. Laws, religious and temporal, only appear absolute when viewed through the narrow lens of one's own era and country. When seen in the broad focus of history they are as changeable as fashions, relevant to the needs of the times. In some Biblical countries abortion was common and permissible. The ancient Jews and Babylonians, however, who wished to multiply and survive, treated abortion as a crime punishable by banishment or death.

These fixed, yet contradictory social and sexual customs of different lands and times had certain characteristics in common. They all had large numbers of sincere and credulous adherents who followed the letter of the law. There were supporters whose motive was profit and there were the usual mindless ones easily persuaded to follow any strong belief. The joiners always allied themselves with the side which was fashionably RIGHT, particularly when it emanated from church and state. And there were the rebels, the heretics who often were the forerunners of a new concept, a new religion or law. Should the new philosophy succeed, then the defenders of the old code would gradually revert to the new.

And of course there were the zealots who denounced all other beliefs as heathen and barbaric.

The early Jews, uncircumcised for many generations, borrowed the practice from the Egyptians, and then denounced the uncircumcised Philistines only to be themselves denounced by Hitler. Today, more than eighty per cent of all Western male children are circumcised as a matter of health. Will the pendulum swing again and the denouncers become the denounced?

So it is with all sexual customs.

It would be absurd to suggest that any one code was the best over a three thousand year period. The test would have to be which code, which morality brought the greatest good to the greatest number of people in their own day and age. A new religion which fits local and contemporary needs can bring confusion and hardship to millions of people when enforced at a later and different period.

There are, today, fiercely respectable defenders of the status quo who are always ready to proclaim that our moral and sexual codes are the best the world and history has known, and all others wicked and immoral. To deviate from this respectable majority is a frightening prospect.

In America today marriage is threatened by elements of a moral dichotomy — love without sex, and sex without love. This impediment to fruitful human relationships evolves from man, separating, in an inhuman way, his ideas of love and sex. He does this to fit a societal pattern instilled in him during childhood. Blindly, he gropes towards unnatural ends, forced on by powerful guilt. In so doing he mutates not only himself, but prepares the way for his children's confusion and guilt.

It is little acknowledged by the blind followers of our social conventions that in the last three thousand years there have been hundreds of deviations from the socially acceptable scheme of things. Laws enforced celibacy (as early as 386-7 A.D.) on the lower clergy while the princes of the church had their concubines and bastard children. The duality of standards, the hypocrisy of prohibiting poor priests to marry while the heads of the church indulged themselves, is forgotten. The license of princes and the aristocracy to have mistresses, lovers, and prostitutes anticipated Machiavelli's "Prince." The guardians of the public morals were ready to pounce upon the slightest suspicion of sensuality and promiscuity of the peasantry. After all, what's the use of being a king, a noble, or titled lady, if you can't taste all pleasures? But when in this age we fall heir to the sexual mores of a nonpracticing church state of a bygone age, that has nothing to do with life in the latter part of the 20th century, then mental sickness, broken marriages and unfulfilled lives cannot be viewed with surprise. These medieval authors of codes, and arbiters of human conduct were not the instruments of the word of God. Nor were they the most noble, unselfish scholars passing on wisdom to a humble peasantry, but clever manipulators, watching carefully over the rights of property vested in the few at the top.

Today we still accept this hypocrisy, and put the seal of God upon it. Religion is full of love. Love will heal the world. Everybody is exhorted to love. And, everyone is confused as to what precisely love is.

When I was a young teenager, I often wondered about the many different kinds of love. There was love of God, love of parents, love of brothers and sisters and love of a girl. This last, of course, was different from the others. There was love for a pet, a possession, a book or toy, love for a friend and love for a teacher — so many types of loves. I recall being told that love for a girl or a wife involved sex, but all other loves were pure and spiritual. No sex there — no sex involving God, father, mother, friend or teacher.

Love is exalted on all sides, in the pulpit, home and in the "good books" and, at the same time, there is a need to control those "nasty" unhealthy feelings of sex and sensuality. I remember puzzling over all these many varieties of love. It was very difficult, but finally I got it. Love for God, parents, friends, teachers was spiritual, clean and innocent, stripped of body feelings and anything personal. The other kind of love was hot and dirty, exciting and wicked. This delicious nasty feeling came from time to time but was almost always suppressed. It had an awesome power over my nice clean senses. In any event, my thoughts and feelings were private — no one could see them. And surely no one else had thoughts such as mine. I remember as a child attending church service and hearing the priest warn the congregation to beware the evils of the flesh, the temptations of the devil, and the hell and damnation that would surely follow such sinfulness and weakness. I knew he was taking about me (but how did he know?), for many wicked ideas had already crept into my head. Even then, I thought it was a pity that such exciting ideas should come under the category of sin. But, I knew I was plunging straight to hell and it would require constant vigilance to reverse the tide so that I might be saved.

It was a tough fight and it grew tougher as the years passed. The devil was surely working overtime to entice me to his evil ways. But in spite of such terrifying pressure, I held on, and finally emerged victorious — and broken! The preacher would have been proud of me. I won my fight with the forces of evil, with the weakness of the flesh. The sirens still shrieked in my ears, but I punctured my eardrums. The summer nights still wove their enchanting smells, but I smothered their fragrance and my sense of smell. With vision I had more difficulty, for the sight of an alluring girl would make my senses reel, but I developed the gift of psychological blinders. As for touching — I avoided touching. I became clever at avoiding contact. I learned if I talked constantly and never listened, I could avoid all contact and warmth with people. I never went into them and they never entered into me. It was a lonely life, but look at the spiritual goals I was attaining. As for taste, that was easy, I simply ate only what was necessary. No self-indulgence, I was a model of proper behavior.

Years later, when I emerged from my trial by fire, I had it licked — I had successfully separated all the various definitions of love into their respective compartments. I acquired the ability of having love for God, father, mother, brother, sister and friend without sensuality, and at the other extremity, I had learned how to have sex without love. And that, I am afraid, is how it came out. Weak mortal that I am. Through the development in my mind of so many august bodies, God, parents, etc., requiring feelingless love, love had to be one thing or the other. Love was for beauty, grace, God and parents. For a woman — there remained only sex. However, if one "loved" the woman, the mighty forces which shaped my understanding of the word love, transported the woman to Olympian heights where she emerged enthroned in grace on the side of God, father, mother — and devoid of sex. I really didn't plan it that way, for I had some conscious understanding in my adult life, that it was possible to have love and sex with one's girl friend or wife. But it was too late. I had been too good a student. I had victoriously evaded the clutches of the devil, and had landed, — straight in hell!

Each person is an island and, privately and silently, carries with him his thoughts, desires, guilts and fantasies. On the outside he portrays the type of person he imagines desirable in society; on the inside, seething and unconquerable, his basic nature boils and churns, driving him into confrontation with the senseless standards thrust upon him by his bewildered parents. The result is chaos. A controlled chaos which elicits in other people the very reactions he dreads. He hides behind a front seeking acceptance and approval, but this false image he projects, brings him rejection thereby reaffirming his own ugly self-image. This chaos prevents him from integrating totally into his own body, into the rhythm and nature of his environment. Sexual confusion, frigidity, fear, failure, marital strife and frequently divorce follow our poor human as consequences of his parents and society turning him away from his natural self.

The strongest exponents of love are usually the loudest opponents of sensuality. But there cannot be and never was any form of love without feelings. And when those feelings strengthen, sensuality follows, and when sensuality grows, sex emerges. People walk in dread of this intrusion; it may lift its head at the wrong time, to the wrong object. People condemn themselves and compound their problems by misinterpreting their natural feelings as manifestations of latent incestuousness and homosexuality.

It is incredible that man, made in the image of God, is made to feel wicked and perverse when his basic nature, given him by God, makes demands.

The teachings of prophets and religious leaders that man goes straight to hell if he accepts his sexual nature as a natural part of life, must have stemmed from their own private fears. These fears were abetted by the belief that unless man exercised tight control over himself he would quickly fall into a quagmire of ancient Roman-type decadence, orgies and bestiality. Strict laws holding man in bondage and guilt speak eloquently of society's distrust and fear of the common man. The authors of such edicts never worried much about the aristocracy. And, while the average man today is as educated as kings and princes of other eras, he is still not to be trusted.

To love is good. One cannot feel truly alive unless one loves. To be close is good; you emerge as a fulfilled person only in a close relationship. To be close and to love opens up the world — everything appears different. Walking becomes an adventure, a meal becomes a feast, and daily life a joy. But one cannot love without running the risk of feelings — and feelings beget sensuality, and sensuality — well, you know, sexuality.

The moral and sexual laws of our time are just as cruel and ridiculous as those imposed upon the happy, childlike people of

Hawaii one hundred and forty years ago, by a band of stern, bigoted, semi-psychotic missionaries from the U.S.A. And, not unlike the brain-washed natives of Hawaii, we are today so indoctrinated with guilt and taboos that we forget how we became that way. We go on responding to that small voice within us. We hold ourselves tightly reined for fear we will run amok — screw everyone in sight. We batten down the emotional hatches holding back feelings and warmth. If we loosen the lid, we fear we may go flying off into outer space and all will be lost.

If one looks at the way we guard our emotions, one might conclude that these strictures were designed for a barbaric, half-human society. Are we so weak, so non-selective, so close to savagery that we can't be trusted to use our potential for rich relationships with other people? The crime against man and society today is that many of our impoverished sex relationships are caused by outdated laws and formulated by bureaucrats with little compassion and no love.

Of all the creatures on this planet, man is the only one who is entirely alone — and yet part of a group. To be fulfilled, man must separate himself and, in his own rhythm, rejoin and feel as one with another human. We must withdraw from the group to examine our individuality, and then, in our own time return. Deviation from this pattern of separating and rejoining results in loneliness and despair or in the complete assimilation of the individual in the mob. A song from "My Fair Lady" puts it "like breathing out and breathing in." All lovers experience the feeling of two halves coming together when in each others presence, and the feeling of being sundered when separated.

Man is not a unit in a mass, moving with blind instinct. He is a separate thinking individual. Yet he is regulated as though he were a member of a flock of sheep. Separate the ram! Tie him up! If he gets loose all hell will break loose!

Our sexual laws, handed down to us over two thousand years by the Judeo-Christian interpreters of human behavior, completely negate man's need to separate and merge. He is programmed to be ashamed if he fuses too closely — so he stays apart. His essential nature struggles within and is constantly suppressed, as a result it frequently emerges in totally unexpected ways.

Man is fearful, on both levels, conscious and unconscious, of being thought latently incestuous and homosexual. We all know of these aberrations but few talk about them for fear of being labeled by association. Yet, millions of readers were fascinated by episodes in the book "Kings' Row," which dealt salaciously with incest in the South.

Because of these fears we freeze our potentially warm natures and shrink from contact with our fellow men and women. Perhaps the most elementary form of this taboo and fear takes place in the very center of life, the family. With millions of children the cry is: "My parents weren't warm or demonstrative towards me — there was very little kissing and hugging in my family." It is strange how we admire the loving and fondling the baby receives from affectionate parents, and rarely reflect on the contradiction of the arms-length stance these same parents express when the baby grows older and enters his teens.

Mother love is exalted in a thousand songs. The sight of a young mother with her baby at her breast fills us with wonderment and joy as portrayed by great masters in countless Madonnas and Child.

What is admired? The picture of love, open, warm and unashamed. Mother and father hold nothing back in their desire to give physical love to their baby. They are not ashamed to touch, pet, and cuddle the infant. Like Adam and Eve in the Garden of Eden, they openly express their natural feelings and the world looks on and smiles.

Yet, in its own way, this act of touching, fondling and caressing could be called, by some literal standards, incest. Did anyone ever define the rule of incest and decree at what age affection and physical demonstration towards one's children is not incestuous, and at what age it is?

What is incest? Does incest mean only the act of copulation between a parent and child? Could incest also mean the holding of certain sensual feelings towards someone in one's immediate family. The mother who cuddles her baby, washes, tickles and kisses him, has him bite her nipples and bury his head in her breast and who hasn't felt a powerful sensuous love, has killed off her capacity to love and will implant this sexual death in her baby. Call it mother love, but it isn't only spiritual and above physical, human feeling. And that is what makes it beautiful. This is, perhaps, the only time in the mother and child's experience together, where all the fears and taboos are swept aside, and love, physical and emotional, come in free, spontaneous play.

It would be ridiculous to imagine a mother loving her baby and, at the same time, avoiding all physical contact. Is this incestuous? Of course not, it is righteously proclaimed. But, by our attitudes towards touching and showing affection to our older children, this most definitely is in the minds of many.

Were it not for our feelings being so private, so unobservable by other people we would not be able to act and react so naturally. If we lit up like Christmas trees every time we noticed feelings of warmth and sensuality, we would be fearful of kissing and petting our babies. And how about the baby? Is he incestuous too? By the extension of adult attitudes, he is. Openly, and unashamedly. Does he seize the nipple only because it means food? Or does he have an instinctive need of his mother's breast because it is soft, smooth and yielding and provides within his body a wondrous feeling of warmth and sensuality? These as yet, unimpaired natural feelings instinctively draw him to his mother's body. A baby is one big sense organ. Its sensuality is not localized in its genitals, but radiates throughout its body whenever it makes contact. It is all innocence and purpose, and we love it for its innocence.

How did we become so uninnocent? The very thought of wanting the warmth and contact the baby seeks so naturally inhibits us and makes us afraid. Were the baby as guilt-ridden and controlled as us he would die. And, as he grows older he slowly will begin to die — not physically, but emotionally.

Before too many years have passed, the erstwhile demonstrative mother and father begin to physically draw away from their growing child. Much is written about man's missing link, but little is written concerning the missing emotional link between parents and young people. You look up one day and everything is under control. What happened in between? Where and how did the change take place? Was it gradual or sudden?

We have been so conditioned that about the only time in man's life when he experiences complete freedom to feel is in early parenthood and babyhood. Why is it so right and innocent at one age and so wrong at another?

Many parents recoil from any demonstration of love towards their growing sons and daughters, fearful and alarmed by the reactions of which their bodies might be capable. In their ignorant, fearful state, they quickly condemn themselves as being potentially perverted and sinful. These parents draw away from their growing children, hold them at arm's length and invent excuses to avoid any sort of contact. Compounded over the years this aloofness becomes unconscious, so the withdrawal is instantaneous at the moment of incidental touching.

Love demands touching. It is all right for museums to say, "Please don't touch the exhibits," but this injunction, applied to humans, spells emotional death. Parents who suffer from this malady become cold and warped. This narrowness and withdrawal dries up the natural juices that once flowed freely in a happier time when the baby was born.

It is natural to love one's children and it is natural to want to demonstrate this love. It is natural to want to kiss and embrace them and it is natural that when we demonstrate our love certain physical feelings may be invoked. This is Nature's way of merging us into the human family.

Unfortunately, like a baby starved of love, so this denial of physical contact will love-starve our older children too. This starving for love is a prime cause of neuroses, psychoses, sexual fears, frigidity, impotence, homosexuality and — unhappy marriages.

Sadly, children wrongly deduce the cause of their parents' coldness and attribute this aloofness to their own unworthiness. They feel stupid, unattractive and unwanted. To compound the problems further they develop traits which, although designed to cover feelings of inferiority, actually call forth hostility and rejection, the very responses, from other people that they dread. While children may condemn their parents privately for their coldness, they condemn themselves more and begin to look with fear and distrust at their growing sexuality.

The surest way to kill off sexuality is to prevent feelings from surfacing. And the surest way to prevent feelings from surfacing is to avoid contact and closeness with other people. The parents' avoidance of warmth with the child becomes deeply ingrained within the child who now begins to resist all intimacy. He has an inner watchdog that forever warns him of the dangers inherent in such "weaknesses."

It is hard to believe that a male and female can have sexual intercourse and yet remain apart from each other. That the act of love with its poetry of physical intimacy can be split into separate parts.

Love can be crippled by guilt-ridden parents but the sexuality of the child will go on. As children mature, their own sexual problems begin to manifest themselves with frigidity in the female and a slackened sexual appetite and detachment in the male. Intercourse becomes one thing, love another. Sex is merely sex, and has nothing to do with feelings, tenderness and love. So man coins certain phrases to express himself: get laid — shack up — get his nuts off — screw. A women is not referred to as a warm, loving partner, but as a lay, a humper, a sex object. Sex ceases to be part of love-making, and becomes a way of measuring one's powers and athletic ability, known as scoring.

Society, seeking to control man's natural instincts, actually create in man the ugliness it wishes to avoid.

You can have sex without love, but you can't have it very good — you cheat your partner and you cheat yourself. You can get laid, score and build up your ego, which will quickly deflate and which will need forever replenishing in this hopeless quest for complete satisfaction. And this, in time, will produce a feeling of contempt for oneself and one's partner; one must go on a sex fast to recharge the sexual battery. Love begets love — sex without love begets satiation. The supreme moment of human contact becomes a dead, disillusioning reaction, the very moment the act is over.

Yet the search goes on. Men and women all hope the supreme gift will reveal itself in the next contact but it never does, hence the enormous appeal of films and novels endlessly idealizing love and lovemaking.

This refrigeration of feelings does not usually occur so strongly in women. Perhaps Nature, being provident, in her design to perpetuate the species, provides women with an intuitive safeguard. In spite of the many inhibiting factors entering into childhood, the female instinctively desires the total love process. She doesn't want the isolated act of sex, but seeks the tenderness and warmth which enhances lovemaking before, during and after the act. Such totality instills not satiation but the seeds of the next union. The male's disinterest in lovemaking, the lack of foreplay, and the speedy return to separate bodies once intercourse is over, is a bitter complaint of most women, married and unmarried.

It is not only Nature which fortifies women in this regard. Mothers are not so inclined to destroy their daughters' capacity to love. Many mothers grow apprehensive when their daughters mature, fearing they are about to be deposed as the desirable female in the house. They become anxious to have the usurper safely married and out of the house. There is an undercurrent of rivalry when females live under the same roof, a fear that the males may become aware of the daughters' growing attractiveness and the wife's diminishing luster. These fears may not be conscious in mothers' minds, but the threat is no less real. Better to keep the daughters' natural instincts and feelings fresh and alive; in that way she will be desirable to another man — outside the house.

With the son, the situation is the reverse. The threat is not inside the house but a female outside the house.

So the best way to destroy the threat is to kill the magnet within the son, which will draw him to the threat. And the magnet is the warmth and tenderness, which was part of the son's equipment when he was born. Sex he will have, but his feelings will be closed off. His sex will not be aroused by his tenderness but rather by occasional basic needs. He will become joined and yet unjoined to the woman he makes love to.

Mothers are amazing. They have such an instinctive knowledge of this process. Soon the male's interest in this new female will slacken and end. She has the same body and he the same needs but he will no longer be aroused by her. So he moves to another female, his sexual interest reawakened. Something new and mysterious. But all too quickly the pattern repeats itself. He imagines he needs an endless round of females to spark him, but his contempt for himself and the female grows with each new experience. He fancies himself a lover but deep down he hasn't the capacity to love and he knows it. He rationalizes his aloofness — he doesn't want to get involved. (I have often wondered whether the word involved could be transposed to *IN VULVA*.) But the involvement he wishes to avoid is a smoke screen for the real involvement his crippled nature so steadfastly avoids. Our Casanova doesn't realize that he doesn't need ten, twenty, fifty or a hundred women to arouse him, that one female to whom he can completely give himself can make him more sexually aware and responsive than he ever dreamed possible. That not only is the sexual experience with this female more abundant, but now parts of his nature come into play that he never knew existed. There is a constant sexual current between them that sparks the whole process of living.

Life takes on a different hue because he is now deeply in tune with his basic nature, with another human being and with his environment. Life is sensuous. A richness and joy bubbles forth in a never-ending flood.

This is all very threatening to the mother of the boy. If another woman can induce such happiness in her son, she might lose him. She can't eliminate all female competition, but she can cripple and atrophy her son's nature, so she — mother — will always be the only woman in her son's life. THOU SHALT HAVE NO OTHER WOMAN BEFORE ME! Tragically this is the design of many mothers whose lives, loves and marriages have been warped. In their bitterness and loneliness they employ such devices to keep forever the one male over whom they have any real power — power induced during his helpless childhood.

So far our hero has conducted his lovemaking in the pattern of Sex without Love. Let's follow him into marriage and see the other effects of this tragic block in his life. His marriage was doomed before it commenced. He had kept his feelings in tight check all these years, he must now continue the pattern. They represent the great unknown! But he must have some feeling for his wife, the woman he is going to marry. He must be "In Love" with her. And that does take feelings. But what type of feelings and where to find them? The girl he marries must not create in him too much lust or the foundation of the marriage may only be sex. Might just as well marry a chippy. No! A sweetheart and wife must be virtuous and full of grace and goodness. So, he marries an angel. There is, of course, some sex — the relationship is still new, but love cannot grow and thrive in an arid desert and it is not long before sex disappears and all that remains is his pure love, freed from lust. Enters now love without sex.

He offers substitutes. Hard work, money, a bigger house and car, a generous insurance policy. But sooner or later, this pure love begins to crumble. Disillusionment is fast approaching, and without sex, warmth and tenderness, strife, dissatisfaction and divorce will follow.

The cure is *not* divorce and remarriage. The problems which plagued this marriage will doom the next. Thus, the miserable cycle is self-perpetuating — on into the next generation.

Trapped in the lonely state of divorce, the ex-wife reacts to the prospect of life without a husband and turns her needs towards her son. Having to live without the warmth and sensuality of a male, she imposes a powerful rein on her nature, for fear it may express itself incestuously towards the boy. This inhibition unconsciously becomes part of the boy's nature adding to his already overburdened fears of closeness and warmth.

When we add the usual nonsense so prevalent in the United States of the sublime, exalted state of Motherhood, and its powerful effect on our culture, the guilt and confusion of this unfortunate young man is all but intolerable.

It is a lapse into madness that a man, who in his business, sets out clearly, definable, realizable objectives, will have no clear cut goals when he decides to marry.

Chapter 8

COME LIVE WITH ME
AND BE MY BRIDE

Wedding bells quicken the hopes of all women, who see in marriage the ultimate goal, the final target, no matter what other ambitions they may have. Men, on the other hand give scant attention to the subject and are content to leave it to some vague distant future. The applause of single women who hear that one of their sex has finally made it "to the altar" is loud — and envious. Seldom does one hear of similar plaudits from the groom's friends.

In "Man and Superman," Bernard Shaw calls marriage the male's greatest tragedy, the loss of his freedom and right to pursue his own life. He admits that the *life force,* as he called it, would inevitably track the male down. In the play, the quarry was eventually cornered and captured by Spanish bandits and . . . by the heroine who followed her target to Spain.

The nuptial announcement portrays a great dissimilarity between feminine jubilation on one hand, and the genuine male concern on the other. However, some time after the wedding a curious change occurs. The reluctant male now wants to stay married, regardless of how conditions may have altered, while the formerly marriage-bent female begins to fret and complain of being trapped. Perhaps the driving desire of females to be wed is an outworn legacy from an age when marriage was considered part of the natural evolution of adulthood. In our present state of marital limbo, out of one era, and not yet arrived at the next, this vestige of female need remains with us somewhat like an appendix. It is there, but has no function. For had it purpose, then the culmination of women's hopes would be happiness instead of disappointment. Yet women complain that marriage terminates their chances of fulfillment and self realization. Why then, in Heaven's name, do they try so hard to enter this confining institution? The spectacle of would-be prisoners clamoring for admittance to San Quentin prison, employing all sorts of blandishments and beguilements to induce some reluctant warden to please let them enter, and then, having been admitted, demanding just as noisily to be released, would indicate some form of madness. The parade of so many women moving heaven and earth to tie the nuptial knot and then straining to untie it is no less ludicrous.

We can divide women into two basic groups. The married and the unmarried. The latter can't wait to get in — the former can't wait to get out!

Ask any lady about to be divorced, if she was in love with her husband when she married him and she will affirm that she was, following quickly with the provision that while she loved him, she was really too young to know what love was. Meaning, of course that she now is older and wiser. This is a charming piece of logic. For it implies that it is possible for a person to be in possession of more faculties and judgmental ability than those that are present at one particular age.

The girl who marries at twenty-five, when divorced at thirty, will say: "I was too young to know what love was." And the one who weds at thirty and divorces at thirty-five will repeat, "I was too young to judge clearly."

These statements suggest that it is possible to have the wisdom and experience of a thirty year old at twenty-five, the discrimination of thirty-five at thirty and the clear selective ability of forty at thirty-five. It actually is an admission that one is too young, at any time, to know what love is, and that the best age to marry is to be at least five years older than you actually are . . . .

I don't believe there is a single life enterprise where we learn so little from past mistakes as in our selection of a mate.

There are two simple but critical questions we fail to ask ourselves prior to signing the high risk marital contract. Nearly all marriages that come to grief are doomed before they start because the contractors neglect to make these basic tests.

One is, our total failure to recognize the fundamental importance of clearly defining our MARITAL OBJECTIVES — Why do we want to marry? We enter the union oblivious to the fact that if we have no real objectives it would be suicide to marry.

Our second sin is our incredible naivety, manifested by our failure to soberly measure, weigh and assess our future partner's preparation and ability to adequately perform his or her role in marriage.

Let's discuss the latter first, training and preparation. In marriage we assume that the bride intends to be a wife — that she will accept the duties of homemaker, mother, and all attendant responsibilities. In short she will handle the domestic side of the contractual relationship. There are, of course, many other facets to marriage, but primarily, the female responsibility towards the home will balance the male's contribution of working and earning a living for his family.

If every individual who contemplated marriage sat quietly alone and asked himself these two simple questions and answered them honestly, more than half the number of marriages would never take place. One doesn't need to marry because one is in love — one can have a love affair. Nor does one need to marry because one is lonely — companions can be found . . . loneliness stems from a lack within, not from a lack without. There are many people, married, and still lonely.

Some years ago I found myself on the brink of marriage. I sat quietly and talked aloud to myself. I asked myself these two little questions. The answers came back loud and clear, no confusion. I did not tie the knot and have been grateful ever since.

A man does not have to jump all the way into marriage to suddenly discover his future wife's preparation for marriage was zilch. Simple observation and common sense would have revealed this to him. We assume he must have spent some time with the lady during courtship and couldn't be wearing blinders all that time. But even if he never saw his bride before they both arrived at the altar, (if such a thing is possible outside India), all he need do would be to examine the typical training and backgrounds of both male and female in our society, as they pertain to the preparation of their future roles.

The male child develops his conditioning towards work during his school years. As his schooling progresses he begins to think in terms of work or career. A gradual adjustment towards this responsibility begins to take place.

Should he leave school early, he may learn a trade, or, if he continues on in college he will select a major that will directly or indirectly lead toward the profession he will later follow. Even his school games orient him toward the team work necessary in a commercial career. He is disciplined, shaped and guided. His ultimate destiny is his entry into his work-role in the future. When he leaves school he accepts the fact that he will work all his life and shoulder his responsibility, for therein lies the foundation of his pride. His ambitions will be centered towards bringing home the pay check and progressing in his work so that he can call himself a SUCCESS.

He will not consider himself self-sacrificing for giving up his boyhood dreams of romance in far off places, of going to sea, or joining the Royal Canadian Mounted Police. He will forget all about following in Gauguin's footsteps who, stifled and unfulfilled as a bank clerk, deserted his wife and children and hied himself to Tahiti, freedom and self expression in art.

Now let's see how the female's training prepares her for her career as wife and mother. Her counter-part role to that of the male.

About the time she reaches her early teens she is well initiated into the art of makeup. The young lady sits in the same classrooms as the young male, exposed to the same subjects.

But the value of an identical curriculum as a preparation for motherhood and homemaking is meaningless. Nevertheless, her education throughout her teens and on through college continues more or less along the same lines as the male.

I am at a loss to know how science, mathematics, history and foreign languages are going to assist the girl in what is going to be the most important role in her life.

If the male and the female are going to make such totally different contributions, why is their education the same? By the time the young lady is 16 or 17, she has learned much about personal adornment. She may have a smattering of shorthand, some typewriting skill, be vaguely grounded in the history of her country, and is dimly aware that Europe lies in an easterly direction. She's probably a good dancer and measures success by the number and variety of dates and invitations to parties. She can drive a car, ski, swim, smoke and has developed some capacity for booze. She is also rapidly succeeding in her ambition to spend as little time as possible at home.

And still there has been no preparation for marriage — none by her parents, none by her teachers and, certainly, none by herself.

Finally, she marries and into this union she brings the sum total of her training and experience. These can be reduced to some proficiency as a stenographer, saleslady, journalist or even computer-programmer. She arrives at marriage helpless and ignorant of the skills she will need. But she does arrive with a disdain for the daily, monotonous chores which are an inevitable part of marriage. The common basics of daily living, cleaning the house, planning meals, buying food and cooking, fill her with indecision and rebellion.

Not only was her training directed elsewhere, but so was her thinking. The fact that she will have to do these chores for the rest of her life never enters her head. One day she feels she will be released from this drudgery. The fact that her husband is always expected to work in no way tempers her thinking.

Frankly, I don't blame her. Were men, educated for a profession or trade, to find themselves suddenly having to assume the responsibility of running a home, they too would recoil and rebel. No less the female. Our culture shaped her perfectly — for something else.

The cornerstone of marriage is the home and it is upon this very rock so many marriages founder. We have come a long way from Plato's Republic where boys and girls were so diligently schooled towards their future occupations and roles. We have it backward today. We train the female to be something for which she was never destined. Would we train a scientist and make him a shoemaker? Would we spend years training an astronaut and make him a hospital orderly? In all areas we are careful to precisely prepare people for a particular craft or profession, but in this most important occupation, we provide none. Worse! We instill in the mind of the female a contempt for the part she will play in marriage.

Should it then come as a surprise that the female recoils from this work and pays only lip service to its responsibilities?

There is an old saw which says that people get the government they deserve. We can follow and say that a husband gets the wife he deserves. For if a woman's training for marriage is ridiculous, then one must declare that the manner in which a man selects a wife is equally absurd. If the male recognizes that the basic contribution he will make to marriage is financial, the fruit of his labors, why then doesn't he carefully measure the qualities of his future wife to assure himself he will enjoy the fruits of her labor?

The male shrewdly assesses the training, experience, attitude and aptitude of anyone he is about to employ to ascertain what quality of production and what type of relationship he will have with that person. *Why then doesn't he appraise the aptitude and ability of his future wife?* Of course, you will smile and say, "I can just see a man asking a girl while he is courting her: Can you cook? Do you like cooking? What training do you have running a home? Does it take you long to clean a house? Are you thrifty? Can you follow a budget? What do you know about raising children?"

The very idea of a man asking such fundamental questions would be considered unromantic — but such prosaic questions are held to be very important by the female. For she carefully appraises the commercial worth of her suitor.

A girl meets a guy, likes him and feels the relationship may deepen. One of the first questions her female friends ask: *"What does he do?"* Not "What is the color of his eyes," but *"What does he do?"* An appraisal. This is most disconcerting if one looks upon the female as more romantically minded than the male.

Should the relationship ripen and the young lady informs her parents, they can't wait to ask: *"What does he do?"* And upon the answer rests the total summation of the man's worthiness by parents, friends and future bride. Years later a wife may complain that her husband's work is no big thing, but in the early stages, his earning ability is his most valuable asset. Here the female carefully follows one of the two rules I laid out earlier: "Her careful assessment — before marriage — of her future partner's preparation and ability to perform his chief role in marriage."

On the other hand, witness the scene when a guy meets the girl he wants to marry. He rhapsodizes about her to his friends; her face, figure and her sexiness. In no way are his male friends going to ask him: "Can she cook? Is she a good homemaker? Has she had any previous domestic training?"

And when the young man tells his family he has found the perfect girl and is going to marry her, can you imagine his parents posing the counterpart question of the girl's parents, which is *"What does she do?"* Meaning not in work, but in homemaking.

The truth is that neither parents nor society devise any plan for the real career the woman will someday pursue. She is not trained mentally or emotionally to be wife and mother. Nor is she trained for a successful career in the business world. Even with a college degree she works on the outer edge of the commercial world. And, if she penetrates that periphery and establishes a career, the possibilities of combining it with a happy marriage are slim. For in this sphere, her relationship and competition with men speedily erode the gentleness and feminity which are necessary constituents in the male-female relationship. Why then is the emphasis placed so heavily on her training to make a living? In what way will it help her in marriage? Or, perhaps this training is a device to provide a form of insurance, a source of income against the seemingly inevitable post-marriage period — divorce?

The second serious consideration ignored in the prenuptial mating dance is: THE SPELLING OUT OF REAL OBJECTIVES. What do they both hope to accomplish, why are they taking this awesome step? There are very few enterprises that achieve success where objectives desired are not clearly perceived and spelled out. In marriage, it seems the only ambition is to be "in love." The epidemic divorce rate proves this, the poorest condition for success.

Love is emotional, marriage is practical; love is romantic, marriage is realistic; love is tender, marriage is tough; love is an art, marriage is a business. The two cannot and do not successfully merge.

The rules of love have been laid down for thousands of years and the prime rule is that when love is over for one, the affair is over for both. The lovers must go their separate ways.

A love affair is not only the least essential factor, in marriage it can be the most damaging. For, the realities and the responsibilities inherent in marriage have nothing to do with love affairs. The daily contact, seeing each other in all moods, and at all times can speedily erode the glamorous picture the lovers once had. Work, the need for money and the demands of a household play the largest part in a couple's life. The arrival and responsibilities of children further sever the romantic ties between the lovers. Children do not belong in a love affair. Neither do cooking and domestic chores, belly-aches, constipation and mothers-in-law. Furniture, car and mortgage payments do little to heighten the vibrancy of desire and tenderness.

Obviously the surest way to kill a love affair is to get married.

What are the objectives of people who marry? In most cases, there aren't any!

Both sexes follow the myth: "They fell in love and lived happily ever after." And that's the whole kit and caboodle. What are the man's objectives? If he wants a relationship with a girl friend, he should live with her. Certainly this is more honest then protesting undying love and marrying her. In fact his love affair becomes more fulfilled in the intimate relationship that exists in living together. No law compels them. Society does not govern their behavior toward each other. They, and they alone, are the ones who decide whether or not to stay together.

There is, of course, the possibility that their love affair will end one day. This supposed calamity when seen in the Cinderella mirror, would appear tragic. But if viewed with the eyes of maturity, the end is not a disaster, followed by anguish and despair. Rather one can say: "I have loved and enjoyed. Now it is over, but I have gained."

"It is better to have loved and lost than never to have loved at all," as Shakespeare said.

Most of us are frightened of enriching relationships. We feel that, if they end, we have suffered a great loss. Not so. In this type of relationship the chances of success are high because the lovers have an objective — to love and live together. An objective to fulfill their love. Therefore they bring into the situation the qualities necessary for fulfillment. They are tender and considerate. They give of themselves and, thereby experience the wonder of love possible only when people are truly open to each other.

It is a lapse into madness, that a man, who in his work clearly spells out certain definable goals, will have no clear cut objectives when he decides to marry. If he wants a lover then let him find a woman he loves and live with her. If he wants a companion, then he doesn't need a wife. If he wants a housekeeper, then let him find a maid — a professional.

But, if he wants a wife he must spell out his purposes. He should concentrate on finding a female who will be the most qualified in helping him realize his aspiration. One who will make a good mother, a wonderful homemaker and a perfect companion. The last three qualities are far more important than the one qualification usually sought — being "in love."

What are the objectives of the woman in marriage? If she seeks a lover, a permanent lover, she is doomed, as many women will testify, to disappointment. Love, as she envisages it, is tenuous and will disappear. If her objective is love then she too, should find a lover and live with him.

Or does the female view marriage as a means of terminating work? The establishment of security? Does she marry because it is the thing to do? I think that the answers to these questions must be yes. I'm sure most women vaguely hope to have children. But I'm sure they are not primary objectives. If they were, why would their arrival spell the loss of freedom and the advent of drudgery.

You cannot train a woman for years to be a singer and then, at the time of her debut, hand her a typewriter and expect her to be grateful. Nor can you train a woman to be a computer-programmer and then expect her to move easily into the role of a wife and perform such totally different work with grace, rhythm and satisfaction. Hope and faith are not enough, and living together in marriage will not create a magic environment in which objectives will be automatically identified and achieved.

This type of preparation — or lack of it — inevitably sows the seeds of dissatisfaction. No wonder soon after marriage women long to get out of the house and get a job.

Women repeatedly declare: "God! Men are lucky to be out of the house everyday, working in an exciting job, meeting people, doing interesting things, being fulfilled." This extraordinary fiction has captured the imagination of many disgruntled married women. They are just as foolishly romantic about the excitement of work outside the house as they were, when single and covetous, about the romance of wedded bliss inside the house.

The truth is that the work most men do is tedious, monotonous and frequently soul-destroying. I doubt if more than five per cent of men find fulfillment in their jobs.

As for our young college graduates, giant corporations fit bright young men (if they are lucky enough to find a job when they get out of school) into their huge, monolithic organizations, so that for the most part, they become anonymous cogs in the wheels of a vast machine. For the sake of security they abandon their creativity and individuality to a lifetime career as company men. These then are the roles of men in the outside world that dissatisfied housewives hope to emulate.

The confusion which plagues women, wanting out when in, in when out, and never finding happiness in either sphere is the penalty one pays for our refusal to grow up and see life as it really is. We prefer to carry into adulthood our romantic dreams of childhood.

In all important endeavors we examine minutely the components of the enterprise and compute the chances for success — except in marriage. We leave that to chance. It is considered not quite the thing to do.

Now let's look at another type of training that is usually omitted in pre-nuptial education — the art of love. The female is not trained to be a housewife, nor is she trained to be a lover. In her formative years she is conditioned away from her natural instincts towards sex by a moralistic culture. Our society, recently lifted out of gloom by removal of some of its iron clad strictures, has not changed enough for us to accept lovemaking as the most natural and healthful of all experiences. The female's warmth and openness, instead of being encouraged and developed, is stifled early. The act of giving, the art of making a man happy, warm and excited, is never part of a young girl's early training. A good woman is not an abandoned woman in lovemaking. A powerful legacy, still with us from centuries of sexual suppression.

The ancient arts of the courtesan, are anathema to the American girl who seems to have some misguided notion that to serve or please a man is to lose freedom and personality. Society does not equip the female to be a wife and mother, nor does it train her as a lover. She is not a good mechanic, nor does she want to be a secretary all her life. What, therefore, is she? Has she arrived at the dead end known as the "lost sex?" The only training it seems the girl receives equips her to be an adjunct to the males' working world.

In some countries the problems of love and marriage are solved in a most interesting fashion. In France for example, the sophisticated Frenchman acquires a mistress, in addition to a wife. The idea of transplanting this noble idea into America would strike chills into our respectable bosoms. Nevertheless, examination will show this arrangement to be not only practical, but a happy one for all concerned.

Unlike the diligent, estimable American male, the French husband leaves his office early, at about three in the afternoon. He has not expended all his energies at work. He still is fresh and very much full of vigor. He arrives at his mistress' apartment. She has had nothing to do all day except create a cozy love nest. She has bathed, fixed her hair, dressed leisurely, and arranged the apartment so that her lover will feel utterly relaxed. A bottle of wine, flowers, music, candles all add to an air of luxury, sensuality and ease. Our hero spends several delightful hours in this exotic atmosphere and, even though he has been married for years, still feels very much the lover.

At about 6:30 he leaves for home where his wife has dinner waiting for him. And now he is truly home with his wife and family. He feels soothed and serene. Should his wife have had a bad day and greet him irritably, he feels abundantly generous and outgoing to listen, to soothe her aches and pains. Soon a pleasant balm settles on the household and the family enjoy their dinner and their evening together.

One's first thought is: "Poor, ignorant, deceived French wife. How could he do that to her? She trusts him and he is cheating her. She works hard all day taking care of the home and the kids and he is with another woman!"

I don't believe that French wives, who are part of this scene, do feel cheated. They understand the situation and know it exists, but they are practical, and strongly motivated. They have objectives which are basically those of being a wife, homemaker, and mother, and these goals are being met. The security inherent in these three most important areas of a woman's life are very important. I doubt if many French wives would change places with the mistress. The life of a mistress is short-lived. It may last a month, a year or more, but it will not endure. I can hear many a American women saying in righteous indignation: "If he spends so much time with his mistress and makes love to her, how much is left over for his wife?"

To this I ask: "How much lovemaking takes place in the average American marriage that has endured for more than four years?" I venture to say the number of times the Frenchman makes love to his wife, in spite of his life with his mistress, exceeds by far the favors carefully doled out by the pressure driven, monogamous, American male.

I have heard American wives say, supposedly in jest, but really in earnest, they wish they could change places, and relinquish the dubious pleasure of homemaker, mother and wife for the exciting role of a mistress.

One fact emerges from the French situation and that is the objectives of the husband, mistress and wife are clear and all handsomely served. We, on the other hand, have no objectives. We want it all. We want our women to be wives, mistresses, mothers, companions, homemakers — everything — and it doesn't work. It would be wiser to marry with clear objectives and hope that love would follow through mutual sympathies, affection and gratitude. One should love the man one marries rather than marry the man you love. (I thought I invented this maxim, but recently I heard it repeated by that most outspoken women's lib leader Germaine Greer, contrary to what is suggested, we *do* agree on some things!)

It is better to have an affair based solely on sex and mutual attraction, with its high mortality rate, than a marriage based upon sex and mutual attraction with its equally high mortality rate.

Marrying for love is as foolhardy as going into the restaurant business because one enjoys eating. The pleasures of eating have nothing to do with a business as complicated as a restaurant, and could indeed with all its attendant problems ruin one's appetite.

The lesson is never learned and each new candidate for marriage marches on, armed only with "that certain feeling" and grossly confused ambitions. The future wife feels fully qualified to be a sweetheart, mother, homemaker, companion and mechanic. Not like the foolish French wife who knows her husband has a mistress outside the home. She is going to be both wife and mistress. She is going to be everything and yet — she is trained to be nothing.

Had she clear objectives, she might be able to curb her fantasies and replace them with practical targets. She would then limit her search to those areas which stood the best chance of attainment. The man she married would be the man most likely to help her achieve these objectives. And this effort would not be ended by marriage — it would be the beginning.

Instead the American female invariably concludes that her goals have all been realized — on her wedding day. Instead of marriage being the instrument by which she can work toward her destination, marriage becomes the objective — the end in itself — the finishing line.

Cinderella prepares her whole life for the ball — to get out of the kitchen, and upon the conclusion of the great day she finds herself . . . . . right back in the kitchen.

The crime of marrying that SWEET YOUNG THING carries with it an enormous penalty. You give her your rights when you marry her, she now gives those rights to a third person, her lawyer. He, well versed in his craft, will now cut and hack into your hide as surely as though you had married him . . . when you married her.

Chapter 9

DO YOU TAKE... THIS LAWYER?

Do you take this lawyer, in addition to your bride, to be your lawfully-appointed mentor, interrogator, persecutor and believe it or not, future partner? You don't, of course. Would you, in your right mind, sign a contract, no matter how favorable it appeared, which gave some unknown attorney the right at any time in the future, to step in and take over? And you could neither fire him nor withdraw.

Suddenly, you find your independence curtailed and your freedom withdrawn as though you had a bad dream and found yourself in the army with all your civilian privileges abrogated. Actually the situation is worse. This partner is your enemy. His particular craft decrees that the more heartless he is to you, the more money he'll make. And, in this nightmare, you have the obligation to pay, not only the booty he will extract from you on behalf of someone else, but his fees for doing so.

And the more brutal he is to you, the higher his fee will be.

This is about as inequitable a pattern of law as you will find anywhere in the world. In what other legal context would you find the abolition of your rights of property, protection and contract? Where else is punishment meted out, emotional and financial, without conviction for crime? And all because a man is foolish enough to "fall in love" and become bound to some sweet, innocent girl — and the attorney, in her future.

The most astonishing feature of this state of affairs is not just its existence, although hundreds of thousands of men have been made to suffer emotional and financial pain at the hands of their wives' attorneys, but that each new applicant for marriage walks blissfully unaware into this onesided and dangerous trap.

The lawyer occupies a unique position in our society. His choice of law as a profession has little to do with his penchant for this craft, his depth of intellect or burning desire to help humanity. It is, rather, the result of his parents' desire to see him cash in on a college education. They hope their selection of this vocation will stamp their son, and by indirection themselves, with dignity and social standing, before he has earned it. It will also, they reckon, pave the way for his entry into politics and business.

All this prestige will automatically accompany his election into that close-knit, exclusive legal priesthood so foolishly venerated by a long suffering public. Our willingness to look up to the holder of a law degree as father, judge and repository of all wisdom, do his bidding, right or wrong, wise or stupid, is typical of our willingness to abandon thought and selectivity in so many other areas of our national life.

Today's lawyer is no expert in all walks of life, despite what we foolishly believe and, contrary to what bar associations would have us swallow. Rarely does a Lincoln, Holmes, Giesler, Bailey or Belli raise his head above the general level of legal mediocrity. The catholic knowledge of today's lawyer is lower, probably, than that of most ordinary businessmen who are, at least, experts in their own fields. The attorney, with the exception of some specialists, is a jack-of-all-trades in the many divisions of law and, were it not for the mystical mantle of legal priesthood, he would be viewed with disfavor rather than reverence.

He has strayed a long way from his early forebears who earned the honor because of their sagacity, reasoning powers, argumentative skill, and oratory, all of which were prerequisites in those days for entry into the legal profession.

It is not my intention to develop a thesis on the history of lawyers, but it should be noted that there is little relation between today's lawyers and the noble precepts which governed the profession in the days when philosophers and orators pleaded cases in the Roman forum. One searches in vain, to find attorneys equipped with the logic, philosophy, scholasticism and integrity which should be the hallmarks of this profession. Instead, the acquisition of a law degree is presumed to endow its holder with all these qualities. In the vast majority of cases it doesn't!

And this individual, who represents your wife in a divorce action, becomes, in reality, your partner. Witness what happens.

Since his attitude to law is based neither on philosophy nor humanitarianism, the attorney has neither the ability nor the desire to try and save your failing marriage. Why should he?

The end of a marriage is something like a death in the family and, at this crucial state, the lawyer should and could stand in the position of a father or a brother. Tragically, his position is more that of an executioner; his actions spell life or death for the marriage.

Compounding further his lack of aptitude is self-interest. His motives are often influenced by his relationship to the large settlements sought in divorce. As a consequence, his function invariably becomes that of a mortician rather than a savior.

There are additional factors which make this type of case attractive to attorneys. Since money, property and estate are the woman's targets in a divorce, the lawyer's assessment of the money involved is rapid; he is thus able to easily compute his share — or, as he terms it, his fee.

Since emotions run high and the spouses at this stressful time, are rarely amenable to reason, the attorney does not have to sell himself on his client's need of his services. The aggrieved wife is ready and eager for his counsel. Furthermore, since his client is giving up her man and is reluctant to seek advice from another male, father, brother or friend, her attorney is in an impregnable position. He is, friend, ally and counselor, and always there to provide her with a ready shoulder to cry on, to assure her she is absolutely right. Where else would a lawyer find so trusting a client?

Now since most divorce actions are settled out of court, her counselor's principal task is to arrange conferences and dole out sympathy. Let her have all the conferences she likes — the husband is paying for them at the rate of from $60 to $100 an hour. He knows that the agony of the husband, the wife and the children, will bring about a settlement sometime in the future. But first let it run its course, inflame it a little, so he can then show how long and painstakingly he has worked to secure the result. Another broken home — another fat fee.

My gall still rises at the recollection of a headline in a California paper: *"Lawyer Wins Divorce for Wife and $5,500,000 Settlement. Lawyer Fee $500,000."* In an interview this proud healer of sick marriages announced his jubilation at his great success. The settlement he obtained for his client was, surely, the largest ever. As for his fee — what attorney could top that. Some victory!

The best weapon in the lawyer's armory is that loose, gap-filled fabric of law known as the matrimony and divorce laws. Since these laws are slanted on the side of the weaker sex (women, not men), it's impossible for the lawyer to lose. The results make American marriage and divorce a joke in the eyes of the world. To the lawyer it is the same story over and over again — unique in the client's experience, but so commonplace to the attorney's jaded ears.

If you are currently facing divorce, let me chart the course of events beyond the range of your emotionally-charged eyes.

Prior to the time your wife has decided to see an attorney we can be sure that one or several of the following preliminaries has taken place:

She has, of course, been contemplating divorce for some time. She has discussed your cruelty, or addiction to TV, or complaints about her housekeeping, or lack of passion, or your perennial tiredness when you come home, with several of her girl friends who always know a *good attorney*. She is convinced that a better life is in the offing — but not with you.

This early phase may go on for some time before the fateful decision is reached. Dressed in her finery (bought by her man)

in leisure time (bought by her man) in the relaxed atmosphere of
a fashionable restaurant (home was never like this) over several
martinis, she recites her litany of complaints with some hard-
bitten female friend who has been through the mill before and
who eagerly seeks recruits to share her own loneliness.

"He said that to you? You took that from him? You let him
get away with that?" On and on, with the man always the
villain of the piece.

Our heroine becomes more and more convinced that she is
right. She is gaining support and her lingering doubts are reced-
ing. The dear friend heaps scorn on this poor, suffering female
for putting up with such nonsense and, at the same time, builds
up the advantages of single blessedness with unlimited money,
independence, and the excitement of being courted by scores of
men. So — this gentle member of the romantic sex suddenly
becomes tremendously objective and businesslike and hies herself to an attorney.

Here the drama follows a precise pattern as though each case
was cut from the same die. Blindly, husband and wife move
along the emotion-charged avenue further and further away from
the possibility of reconciliation. Unless she is particularly unfeeling, the wife is somewhat tremulous and uncertain as she
awaits her first appointment with her new attorney. The die is
almost cast.

She feels she should do this — and yet — it is hard to think
clearly. If only there was someone to think for her. Her
husband? No, he is the enemy. Who then? It must be a man.
Which man? So much hinges on this enormous step.

The door opens.

Lo and behold here is a kindly, sympathetic male face —
intelligent, warm and deeply interested in her. And he belongs
to the honored brotherhood that all her life she has been trained
to trust. He knows all — the law, the code, the morality. It
never crosses her mind his opposite number in court is always
hell-bent on proving him wrong. The office is peaceful in

contrast to her turbulent mind. Here is a book-lined sanctum; hundreds of books, each volume ready to spring forth and proclaim her lawyer is right when he says she is right!

She has left home — and she has come home.

Who is this man who holds the fate of your marriage in his hand? A lawyer, yes, but what kind of man is he?

He may be wise, decent and understanding of this most critical problem. He may have his own family and reflect: "There, but for the Grace of God, go I."

He may not want his livelihood to depend on such total misery and may earlier have decided to use his unique position to do something for society's ills. Some attorneys have turned their backs on large fees and have been instrumental in bringing husbands and wives together. But such nobility is rare in this money-oriented culture.

Arbitrator, counselor and doctor of human suffering — this is what our bewildered couple needs but, unfortunately, there are too few of these men. Instead, most attorneys are inept, rapacious and heartless. Your chances of meeting a good one are infinitesimal. From here the road away from marriage goes not quickly, but rather slowly and surely to hell.

You enter the room. You sit down. You confront a pleasant looking man. You are about to take your life out of your husband's hands and put it into the hands of this stranger; out of the hands of the father of your children, the man you have lived and loved and slept with.

Your husband you know — so you don't trust him. This stranger, possibly cruel, greedy and stupid, you don't know — so him you trust.

Where to begin? In retrospect, your complaints seem almost petty. It all is so tangled and disjointed.

Take your time, he encourages, "Why don't you start at the beginning?" Why not, if it helps you and fertilizes his fee. This is probably the only occasion, in a matter of law, where the client doesn't anxiously watch the clock in fear of the money being spent. Isn't it wonderful? This release from such considerations on such a bewildering occasion. And there's no husband urging you to be careful of costs. Hubby is no longer the man in charge — he has been replaced by this kind, considerate and understanding new friend.

You begin your story, usually somewhere near the end, pick up the middle and travel quickly to the end again.

Then you start again, this time at the real beginning, talking earnestly and convincingly — somehow you must persuade this man you are right, as though you were in court and your listener, the judge. Your emotions well up, tears overflow. You are relieved to find this man so perceptive and patient, a new experience for you. You had almost forgotten that a man could be so understanding.

The contrast between this silent, deeply concerned male and your argumentative husband convinces you, you are on the right track. You relax and recollect incident after incident which support your position. On and on you rush into the new relationship you are building with this warm, concerned man. Further and further you are moving away from your husband and nearer towards this stranger who is on the threshold of becoming your business partner.

All your life you have tried to see both sides of a story. You have been told that when there is emotional stress you should guard against bias in your point of view, but all this is forgotten now. The principles of objectivity and compassion are bypassed and this sober, mature gentleman who sits opposite you makes no effort to check this disastrous plunge into emotionalism.

This is a rare and pleasant experience for you. Actually, you are being encouraged to continue in this tantrum by a very important man, a very apostle of right behavior and an interpreter of conduct and law. Your doubts are swept away.

You grow strong and more sure. You were right all the time! This clever man is saying so.

Suddenly you realize you have been talking for more than three hours. The time has gone so quickly. You apologize. How thoughtless to take up so much of this clever man's time. He must be clever, look how silent he has been, except on the few occasions he has gently prodded you to go on. You rise.

Somehow you feel different — stronger. Your crumpled body is straightening. A curious thing happens as you prepare to leave and pull on your gloves. You become aware of your clothes, your hair and your person. For the first time in a long while you feel like — like a young girl. This fancy is heightened by the warm, friendly handshake as you reluctantly leave your new ally. The journey home is a new experience. Dawn is breaking, the adventure has begun. Only now you are not alone, you have a partner. He is on your side. This new man is going to take over and make everything right.

So ends phase one of the Headlong Flight Into Misery.

There are some things our heroine does not know. What she interprets as sympathy and approval is really just the tools her attorney uses to ply his trade. It has nothing at all to do with the justice of her case. The circumstances, however, make the seduction profitable and useful to both sides. She can have her fling — at great cost to her later — and he has his client securely on the hook.

We treat attorneys as though they were just and objective. They are not. Most of them are tradesmen wearing legal mantles.

Were it not for emotionalism, and the consequent lack of reason experienced in conflicts, business, marriage and the thousand-and-one relationships which make up the human scene, the majority of lawyers would not be needed. Unreasonable childish behavior is at the foundation of most legal actions. Eventually reason does — has to — prevail through court action or attrition and the accumulation of huge legal fees. The tragedy is that the same result could have been achieved without the tremendous output of time, money and nervous energy. But, being human and infantile, we want to enjoy our anger, so we do the lawyers' bidding.

He, in turn, has a deep understanding of this aspect of human behavior. He knows he can't depend on the more prosaic part of law to earn his living. He needs the human conflict to maintain his income.

There is a wonderful story attributed to Abraham Lincoln when he was a young lawyer in Springfield. A wealthy businessman strode into Lincoln's office one day with blood in his eye. A poor shopkeeper owed him $2 and was not going to pay up. He, therefore, wanted Lincoln to bring an action against this man. Lincoln tried to dissuade this important gentleman, but to no avail. It wouldn't be worth it, he told the client. It would cost more than the debt and the struggling storekeeper might not even have the $2. The big man persisted. "It is the principle of the thing." he boomed, "The principle of the thing."

Lincoln saw that reason had departed, so he sighed and took the case and told the client the fee would be $10. The client paid and left contented. Lincoln then went to the debtor, gave him $2 to pay the debt and shared the remainder with him, $4 apiece.

Justice was done! Lincoln's client was happy, Lincoln was happy, and so was the poor shopkeeper.

The situation hasn't changed much. The attorney knows, when a new client enters his office, that an emotional upheaval is in progress. He knows that, to cement his relationship with the client, the latter must feel that he badly needs the services of a lawyer. Since most problems can be solved with reason and a little compromise by the parties, these are the last ingredients the lawyer wants to use at this time — particularly in the marital stew.

Therefore, the agitated client is encouraged in her grievances. "Did he do that to you? Oh no, he can't get away with that — I don't see how we can lose in court." This is the first time the lawyer uses the plural personal pronoun — there will be many more before the blood begins to spill.

There is a curious reluctance to ask the attorney how much his fee will be. How can such a question be asked of someone who is your friend, your partner? His cooperation, talents and interest at this juncture, go far beyond something as crass as money.

At this critical time, you are a child in an adult body and the attorney knows what you want and is delighted to give it to you. You want sympathy — he gives sympathy. You want confirmation — you get it. You want a father — he becomes one for the asking. You want judge, jury and an impartial authority to say: "You are right." You get these too. What an incredible satisfaction.

For the first time in your dilemma you feel relieved. Like Lincoln's client, you leave the office, content. You are also on the hook — wed now to the attorney, and your adolescent emotions are the basis for the contract. The attorney skillfully uses your symptoms to support your conviction, "You need a good attorney." Later it will be a different story — "Settle, compromise, be reasonable, you may get less in court — there's always that chance." Besides, later your childish emotions will have run their course and you'll be only too happy to have done with a growing nightmare. In many cases where the husband contested in court, the wife received considerably less than was offered in the prior negotiations.

Many women enjoy the opening gambit of this drama. There is a powerful desire in most of us, when our emotions take over, to prove that it was the other guy who was at fault, who hurt me, "I was the good one — I never did anything wrong." While there is some temporary pleasure in this rationalization, unnecessary pain and suffering follows as a consequence.

At this point, our heroine is indeed a heroine, the central figure in an emotionally-packed drama. Quite a different person from the prosaic housewife doomed to boredom, marital strife and hubby's indifference to sex.

All her life, many of her desires were held in check by the limitation of money. Now all this is changed, the ceiling has been lifted. Her friends say, the law says: "Spend what you like. The brakes are off. The old man must pay." She is a free agent and the law, in the person of her attorney, is her partner. Together they will show her husband where he gets off.

The bull has been set loose in the china shop. Suddenly, the care and the economy the husband has exercised to build the family estate is swept away. The wife now, literally, is in control. She can draw on his account, even his business account. She can hamstring him, tie him up in knots. The law and her attorney says so. She really enjoys this role. For years she was ambivalent as to whom was the weaker sex, and the meaning of equality had been so difficult to grasp. She dwelt in some sort of twilight zone neither masculine, nor feminine. Now she is no longer uncertain; equality has been achieved with a bang. The shackles are off and she is free. The freedom of the sexes has been won.

There is a cost for all this — but it will come later. For all this is purchased at the price of her attorney stepping more deftly into her husband's still-warm shoes. She hardly notices the increased use of the *we's* and *our's* her champion employs, and if she does, she enjoys the feeling of support and solidarity. What was previously the estate of her husband and herself is now becoming the estate of herself and her attorney, controlled, at least temporarily, by him.

Selfishness and stupidity enter the picture. In the past, she and her husband saved, invested with care and watched their estate grow. Now all this has gone by the board. The voice in her ear tells her to look out for herself or she'll be left behind.

In divorce cases where there are tangible assets, and that applies to most families whose income is $20,000 or more a year, money, estate and alimony are the targets. Divorce is easy enough; any reason will suffice — the wife hardly needs an attorney. It's the cash that forms the basis for the wife-lawyer alliance. The more she gets the more he gets. So what? It all comes out of the husband's hide anyway. Conscience? Well, he's only doing his job and helping his client. She said her husband was a brute.

It's amazing how the law has sanctified robbery on such a large scale. It smiles benevolently on license to plunder. And the attorney for the wife goes smugly about his business secure in the knowledge that he will have access to and a share in the husband's money. She and he will win — the law says so.

Soon after the wife's first meeting with her attorney a new phenomenon occurs which baffles the hell out of the husband and adds to his bitterness. The sweet gal he married has suddenly turned into a calculating, unrecognizable, heartless shrew. Her unreasonable demands, her estimate of what he can afford, her indifference to the freezing of his business funds bears no resemblance at all to the girl he used to know.

He can't reach her to talk or reason. She has turned into a pillar of salt. How can such a transformation take place? Was she always a bitch, did he never see it before? Lawyers advise clients not to meet and discuss the case with the other party in their absence. While this may be a valid procedure in other legal actions, it effectively seals off all chances for dialogue and conciliation in a divorce action.

As the misery continues, month after month, the bitterness reaches deeper into the husband's bones as he ineffectively tries to meet with his wife. She is implacable. He now hates her with a vengeance. His own emotions are rampant. She now becomes the enemy. The problems and anger of their married life were minor compared to his mounting anger and frustration. No one has ever treated him with such cruelty. This is total war. And he has to toe the line, jump on command, pay out large sums at her bidding everytime she cracks the whip.

One poor wretch I know, after 15 years of marriage, found himself heading for divorce. His wife changed from a decent human being into a snarling tigress — so much so that her venom actually boomeranged.

The husband had, with great care, built a small estate. He was particularly skillful on the stock market and, at this time, was aware that the market was going to tumble. He pleaded with his wife to let him sell the stock. She remained firm. The stock market became a shambles and suddenly $80,000 worth of stock became worth $20,000. She showed him!

How does a normal woman become, overnight, an unfeeling, cruel stranger? This is a mystery that baffles many men. The sources of the transformation are so effectively concealed that men can only conclude that their wives must have been always like that, but they just didn't see it before. The hopes the husband had for reconciliation have now gone. She is the wicked adversary and he wants to hurt her as much as he's been hurt. So he engages an attorney, and is full of plans to strike back and punish.

An almost similar situation now exists between him and his attorney as that between his wife and her lawyer. The husband's original concern about expenses is gone.

But the husband's disregard for costs has come too late and for the wrong reasons — anger and revenge. Many men on being served The Order To Show Cause after the wife files for divorce, are convinced that they can talk their wives out of this madness and do not hire an attorney right away. To do so would be an acknowledgment that the marriage was doomed. Subsequently, when eyes and heart reluctantly accept the truth, they hesitantly engage a lawyer.

There is a strange conflict of behavior at this state. The wife, not a business person versed in the wisdom of the axiom, ''You must spend money to make money,'' now realizes full well the importance of this rule and is prepared to make a large outlay (her husband's).

The husband, good businessman though he may be, initially regarded the expenditure of money on attorneys with anxiety and shops around for a lawyer whose fees are low. This is a serious mistake. The husband should immediately select the finest attorney, regardless of cost. He should treat the outlay as a business investment, for such it is. Money saved on a lawyer in this struggle will cost him many times more in a bad settlement obtained by an inept practitioner.

The factors which might have overcome this crisis — charity, understanding, and compromise, are now hopelessly buried. The hope of maintaining some sort of a reasonable relationship for the sake of the children, is utterly lost. Forgotten too, are the original causes of friction; like mad automatons, the contestants act and react to each new agression, compounding the hurt, the spite and the hatred.

The pot is boiling steadily, slowly rising to its correct critical temperature. A little more fissionable material, and it may be ready. Meanwhile, a year or two of unspeakable misery has passed.

How did they get like this?

How did the wife become so inhuman, so strong?

Soon after the wife's first appointment with her lawyer and soon after he has probed the extent of her husband's earnings, savings, real estate and holdings, ostensibly for her sake, "for some of these husbands conceal their assets, you know," but really for his own, the lawyer feeds the information into that special mental computer he always has ready. It shows him at a glance — so much money, so much in stocks and bonds, so much real estate — divided by so much time and hatred, conflict and emotion, will deliver with absolute certainty, a sizeable fee.

The legal friend now begins to take over. The *we's* and the *our's* have jelled into a close-knit partnership. The lawyer begins to outline a strategy which might be synthesized into.

The more she gets, the more he gets; the longer the fight — the more he gets; the harder the fight — the more he gets; the uglier the contest — the more he gets.

Ugly fights need unreason on both sides and total mutual cruelty. Hard fights need confusion and the compounding of problems until they seem insoluble. Long fights require opposition to meetings and arbitration. Big demands beget strong refusals.

Such is the order of combat in the divorce arena. As the plan unfolds, some wives, after the initial emotions are spent, are aghast at the hardship they are urged to inflict upon their husbands and question the need for such strong measures.

And this is the big one, the last bridge for her attorney to cross. Once over, the rest is smooth sailing. It is precisely at this crossroad that the normal wife turns into a virago.

As long as she lived with her husband, despite differences and quarrels, they had a common purpose, marriage, home, children and future. They pulled together because when one was hurt so was the other and when one was engulfed in crisis the other had to step in and help if only for his own sake. But all this changed once the wife engaged an attorney.

To assess the terrible cost of a divorce which reaches the stage of acrimony and execration, let us look at what could and should be done when serious marital difficulties begin to make themselves evident.

Two important targets should be identified. One is reconciliation and an understanding of the problems which led to the rift so that such pitfalls might be avoided in future, and the marriage more securely anchored; or — a divorce with as little friction as possible. It is important in such a case to salvage some sort of friendship for the sake of the children. Inevitably, the parents will meet many times in the future to discuss problems and decisions affecting the children. It is desirable that the atmosphere at such meetings be harmonious, for you can't go running to the attorney every day after the divorce is granted. Eventually, it would be hoped, the trauma of the divorce will disappear, and when the parents meet in the presence of their children, they will not be snarling at each other.

There is no doubt that love and hate are akin and that we can hate more strongly those we once loved and by whom we feel we have been hurt. Unfortunately, the wife's counselor uses these converted emotions to further his own ends.

Many wives are shocked at the strong measures proposed by their attorneys. Even though they feel their husbands were guilty of reprehensible acts, they don't want to butcher him. Some women recognize they are hurting themselves and their children by such devastating tactics and are destroying any chance of future relationship, let alone jeopardizing the husband's earning ability.

But our legal friend is ready for this turn of events. At the first recoil and remonstration on the part of the wife, he indicates that such measures are unfortunate, but necessary. He reminds the wife that she is a woman, weak and helpless, and that he must use *all* methods for her protection. He imparts to her an exaggerated sense of helplessness and finally makes it clear that she must choose between himself, her friend and counselor, and strong measures which, after all, are designed only for her protection, and her estranged husband with whom she is locked in combat and who will, given half a chance, cheat and deceive her.

There is only one way she can possibly go. Having severed her reliance on her husband, she cannot return to that indecisive land between husband and attorney. So, reluctantly, she consents and battle is joined.

Now follow the edicts, injunctions, court orders, summonses, complaints, interrogatories and depositions. And, while her signature attends these documents, the true mover is the attorney. He is doing what he wants to do. He now has the power.

"Do you take this attorney to be your lawfully appointed partner, in all your wife's legal rights — to answer and obey his writs and demands, to harass and to question you, to punish and to bleed you?" And you can't cry: "Stop!"

Step back a moment and look at this extraordinary situation. It almost defies description.

As long as you remain single, you are a free agent. And he, the future attorney must remain silent; he can do you no harm. He can hardly address you. You fall in love and, while you court your fiancee, you are still free individuals, each protected by equal laws. You marry, and automatically you abrogate your rights and freedoms. Some years pass and for some reason or other, your wife seeks a divorce; immediately, you come under the authority of a powerful, one-sided law.

This severe penalty extracted from you because you dared to get married, firmly suspends the sword of Damocles over your head. Your wife now seeks to exercise the rights you gave her. You gave your rights to her when you married her, she gives those rights to a third person, her lawyer. He, well versed in his craft, will now cut and hack into your hide as surely and as legally as though you had married him — when you married her.

I am amazed that any man ever has the nerve to marry!

Time passes and the wife has settled down to a routine of visits with her lawyer. The tug-of-war is in full pitch and the attorney is now master of the situation, of his client and of you. His demands are heavy and the justification for ever-larger legal fees grows daily.

There is another interesting act to this drama. The attorney is banking on his sure knowledge that most husbands will eventually agree to an inequitable distribution of alimony, child support and community property assets in the wife's favor.

After a year or more of being bled emotionally and economically and after arriving at the conclusion, often erroneous, that the hardness of the lawyer is a reflection of his wife's attitude, the husband decides to get out of the nightmare. Contracts are drawn and a date is set for the hearing. The husband agrees not to attend, and another mockery is made of the law by the husband's default.

He defaults in marriage, during divorce and he defaults in court.

Does the man have equality under law? He does not. What really is in contention in a contested law suit is — money.

Does the man have the desire to earn more money during this period and share it with his rapacious opponent? Of course not. Would a man share the fruits of his labor with his enemy?

Witness his dilemma. Through her attorney the wife makes the most outrageous demands — demands that could cripple him for life. Perhaps the husband has been cheated. The wife may have conspired with a lover, cheated in adultery, or deliberately created a scene so that the provoked husband gave the necessary grounds of cruelty for divorce. And perhaps the husband has proof of all this. What can he do? Nothing.

Sure, he can go to court, and chances are that he'll win, but the wife will still get the home, kids, community property and alimony. When the crippling cost of winning begins to dawn on the husband and he adds the temporary alimony he'll be paying from six months to two years, plus both lawyers' fees, cost of depositions, interrogatories of both sides, plus the possibility of developing more community assets, which he'll have to share with the wife, he'll sue for settlement quickly.

And in addition, he has had months of emotionally-charged hell. So, its cheaper to cough up quickly and get the hell out. Since the right to go to court is designed to protect both parties — in this case from an excessive demand for money — the act of exercising this right may hurt as much or more.

One more piece of cruelty on the part of the state. The state decrees that if a wife should seek divorce and there are community property assets which might protract the divorce proceedings, the husband must abstain from sex for that indefinite period. The penalty for slipping is the possible loss of his share of the community assets.

Now who ever cooked up this piece of brotherly love? Compared to this punishment, the pillory and stocks were mere slaps on the wrist. Apart from his physical and emotional needs which continue law or no law, there is no time in a man's life when he has greater need for warmth and reassurance from a woman than during the black divorce conflict.

Some divorce lawyers, to compensate for the expensive screwing they give the husband, favor the wife with one for free.

But, the wife has won. Her partner, the lawyer has done the trick. Soon she will be without husband and, without her ally, the attorney. In a year or two she will discover, as have so many woman, that other men are not so attractive and faultless as she supposed. She will find that her former husband had as many good qualities and, perhaps, fewer bad ones, than the men she is now meeting. Soon she will start approaching ex-hubby for a reconciliation. But hubby, like a defector from Russia, tasting freedom for the first time, will not be inclined to return home.

But, it is all over now. The heart-rending drama of a sundered family has been seized upon by a member of the great legal profession who entered the scene as full partner, but with none of the responsibilities of a husband. He played his part, fanned the flames, took his pay and departed as silently as he came, back to anonymity where he should have stayed in the first place.

For him the case is closed. But for the sufferers in this misery, the husband, the wife, and the children, the agony goes on.

At times of marital stress, there is a need for a strong, impartial person to intervene, arbitrate, calm emotional upheavals and restore objectivity and common sense. A need to gain the confidence of both parties, to separate the issues from the subjective distortions. To weigh and measure and reveal to both parties the realities of the problem. There is a need to advocate compromise and achieve either reconciliation or, at worst, a friendly agreement to divorce and settlement.

If there was ever a time when such an agency is needed, it surely is at the threshold of divorce, but where can it be found? Nowhere. Marriage counselors are untrained for this phase of the marital relationship and inadequate in the face of the strong temptation presented to the headstrong wife by the law and lawyers.

Psychologists and psychoanalysts are too few and too expensive and their treatment too long and involved to be effective before the patient succumbs to his marital wounds. Priests and clergymen certainly have not stemmed the tide of divorce.

There is a need today for people skilled in negotiation, salesmanship and psychology, whose love of humanity motivates them to play the part of mediator.

The use of lawyers in divorce is dangerous and enormously costly to the principals and to the nation. Changes in our style of living and sense of values over the past 60 years make divorce an almost inevitable consequence of marriage today. It must be acknowledged that the epidemic will continue unabated. Steps, therefore, must be taken to cope with a situation which is part of our daily life. We can no longer view divorce with surprise and dismay. It is here to stay.

A major effort must be made to replace today's ugly, tortuous and archaic system with something new and beneficent. And this means the training of a group of new professionals, negotiators, arbitrators and middlemen. Enjoying the trust of both husband and wife, they would soothe rather than inflame, advocate reason rather than emotionalism, trust rather than skepticism and compromise rather than inflexible, impossible demands.

Lawyers are the worst professionals to handle this epidemic. Apart from the fact that their training in no way teaches them to be negotiators, salesmen and human counselors, the nature of their profession and their place in law militates against their effectiveness, even if they had those attributes. Adversary procedures are, no doubt, the best method of seeking the truth in a court of law. Both sides are well represented by counsel, and adversaries they are, but this professional legal method, the basic component of lawyer usage, has no place in an impending divorce action; it is dangerous and highly destructive to the parties concerned.

Lawyers set themselves up as negotiators. They are not! Through representing their clients, they become principals. Webster and Oxford Dictionaries define a negotiator as a middleman — a party who seeks to earn the trust of *both sides* — who neutrally arbitrates fairly and equally both sides. This man works to remove suspicion, anger and recrimination, and replaces them with trust, good will, compromise and settlement.

Since the urgency is so great, it calls for a revolutionary new approach. A new profession of marriage doctors who can be called in to use proven talents to heal and restore health, or if this is impossible, to use surgery as a last resort as painlessly as possible. Surgery with the best anesthetist where the patient recovers quickly, with the least damage to himself and to other members of his family, and their future happiness.

FOOTNOTE: . . .

Although this concept is more than a decade old, I recently had occasion to put it into practice. Called in to mediate between two friends who had decided on divorce after years of strife, I was able to sit down with both of them and, in three hours, painful perhaps but pervaded by the spirit of reason and friendship, work out an agreement which covered the division of family assets, alimony, child support, visitation rights and several other contingencies designed to reduce friction and smooth the path toward future friendship.

Without warfare and reciprocal accusation, the couple faced the realities of their situation. They decided on a period of reconciliation but this did not work, so they went ahead with the divorce agreement which was based on the original document.

The agreement was submitted to a lawyer who checked it for omissions. Finding none, he transposed the document into legal language. Incidentally, this same lawyer had just concluded a bitter divorce action which had lasted for 18 months. At the meeting I arranged in his office for the signing of the documents, he was astounded at the spirit of reason and even amiability which prevailed between my friends. He agreed that the signing of the divorce papers after a token court appearance, will be as free from trauma and pain as it is possible to make it.

In this instance, not only were the principals able to settle this painful matter harmoniously and with small cost, but their child was spared the endless argument and hostility characteristic of most divorce actions.

Total time spent — three hours initially in the couple's home; agreement reached and initialed by both parties. Lawyer converted document into legal language — 30 minutes. Meeting of couple and self in lawyer's office — 20 minutes. Less than four hours from start to finish.

It does work!

There is a powerful resistance on women's part to behave like women; to be feminine and submissive is equated with weakness. Men, on the other hand equate the masculine traits of aggressiveness and strength with roughness and bullying.

Chapter 10

THE SINS OF THE FATHERS. . . AND THE MOTHERS

I have spent a lot of time talking about the behavior of adults, married and unmarried, and the effect that custom, society and materialism, with their adverse influences on real values, play upon these candidates for divorce. Let's examine the effect of these values on our children, the brides and grooms of tomorrow.

It takes little imagination to envisage the influence broken homes and embattled parents have on the normal growth of the young. For here the pattern is set. Here is conceived admiration or derision for the antics of their so-called betters, the adults.

On we go in our blasé way, telling our children what they should and should not do oblivious to their faintly concealed contempt.

It is easy to condemn the young for their lack of respect yet we carry on as adult delinquents. Their everlasting concern with fun may appear shallow in our eyes but are our values deeper?

Idealism is a characteristic of youth. College students everywhere are out to change the world; the young are instinctively on the side of the good. Picture then the shock, and despair, that must becloud these young minds during the ugly period preceding and following divorce.

Honesty and integrity are qualities we wish to implant in our youngsters but our way of life spells our own superficiality; from the staggering divorce rate to the boasts and lies we blisfully accept on TV and radio. From the obsession we have to accumulate more and more possessions, throwing away still usable goods, to the national propaganda print-machine which pre-fabricates public opinion.

In the home, school and church, the child is taught to be truthful and trusting, to look for the good, not the bad. He is taught to think before punching out, to use reason, and common sense. He is taught that it is childish and vulgar to boast about his parents' possessions, cars, homes and wealth. He is taught to be sportsman-like, to be a good Christian, a good American, a good scout — and he wants to be all this.

How then, does he reconcile the childish, savage attacks our politicians make upon each other, and on other countries that are temporarily out of favor? Christ said: "Love thine enemy." How does the child fit this into his developing concepts? He does not realize, as do few of his elders, that America's Holy War against Communism was not a fight against an ideology, but a chess move in the old struggle for the Balance of Power. We have had these crusades before in different guises. Whenever the need arose in state or church to mobilize the population, means were found to persuade the people to cast aside reason, tolerance, and even Christianity. There were the Holy Crusades which gave the stamp of legality to rape, violence and plunder. There was the Holy Inquisition, conducted in the name of Christianity, which for horror and brutality would make pagan sacrifices appear humane. More recently we had witch hunts and the burning of witches and many a God-fearing lady and gentleman boasted of their ability to recognize real witches.

Since governments suspend reason as a matter of expediency, it is hard to expect children not to follow suit. There has hardly been a day since the end of the last war when we haven't screamed hysterically at the ungodliness of the Russians and the insolence of the Chinese. Our penchant for hurling abuses on the former legal governments of countries like the Dominican Republic, Chile and, not too long ago, North Vietnam, have become an obsession with us. If Russia proposes something that seems to make sense we search for ugly motives. We manipulate the news to suit us best and we behave in the self-same manner in which we accuse the communist nations. We say they are atheistic and materialistic — we are God-like and spiritual! What can our children think of all this? They are being taught to behave one way and shown another.

The cold war with Russia endured for eighteen years, and all during that time we told our children to discard pettiness and act more maturely. Yet our own behavior to out-of-favor countries was childish and dangerous. We tell our children not to be infantile yet we act psychotically! Their behavior could result in a bloody nose; our international antics could precipitate an atomic holocaust.

Our double standards are dangerous and the price of our expediency is the destruction of our children's trust and belief. The Machiavellian policy of governments in moving whole populations at will, to love, and then, to hate, is rarely commented upon by parents, schools and churches. During the Russo-Japanese war we favored the Japanese, so the Japanese were heroes — and the Russians monsters. Then came World War I. The Russians were heroes up to 1917 the year of the revolution, the Germans monsters and the Italians were brave. In 1942 the Russians became heroes again, the Germans monsters, the Japanese murderers, and the Italians were jackals. After the war the switch was thrown again. The Russians became monsters, the Germans hard working and industrious, and the Italians craftsmen and artists. And the Japanese? Why, they arrange flowers and play with fans.

The switch is being thrown again and the Russians have become our partners in space and the cloak of darkness which fell upon 700 million Chinese people for twenty years is now being lifted as American corporations scramble to Red China in search of business. Who next will be elevated to sainthood or condemned to the devil?

All this talk about the communist threat is bunk; we support communist or fascist governments whenever it is in our own interest, to wit — Yugoslavia and Spain. We are not against dictators: witness the dictators and governments we support in

Latin America, the recently overthrown junta in Greece, the military regime of Chile, and President Park in South Korea.

However, it is unwise for governments to tell their countrymen they must be for or against another country because of the government's need to manipulate the balance of power; the people would not buy that. There must be an ideological call to duty — St. George and the Dragon, and we are always St. George. And the Dragon? Whoever might tilt our position of power.

At the advent of Christianity, Augustus Caesar regarded this new religion with dismay. The Christians were tearing down the old and true institutions of the State. Their contempt for the Roman Gods threatened to undermine the economic foundation of Rome. They were revolutionaries and atheists according to pious, Godfearing Roman citizens; they were even communistic with their concepts of brotherly love, their sharing of goods and indifference to material possessions. (I wonder how many Americans today would have been on the side of the Romans in those days?) Yet the world learned to live with these two ideologies. The two civilizations influenced each other enormously. No one can read Marcus Aurelius, a so-called Pagan Emperor, without being struck by the man's charity, humanity and "Christianity."

There was a time when the world was convinced it could not contain a Christian and Mohammedan world. Bloody wars were fought to prove it. But they did learn to live together. On each occasion a way of life is threatened, adjustments are made and peace reigns again. For perhaps the first time in history, our recent holy war — against the communists — is boomeranging back on our own population, our children.

Advertising has become a way of life with us. The campaign becomes more important than the product. Advertisers shriek, flatter and seduce us to buy their products. If Hitler could have conquered a nation of 80 million people through radio, newspapers and repetitive propaganda, think what he could have done today using modern advertising methods and TV. How can children grow up with any concern for truth, subjected as they are to the endless barrage of advertisers' lies? What is important, the merchandise or the integrity of the young?

The adult may smile at the transparently-false claims for the best brand of cigarettes, the finest soap, the longest lasting tires, the best cars, and close his ears to the huckster's snake-oil, but what about the child? He absorbs it all. He looks at his parents to see how they receive this vulgarity but he sees no disapproval; rather he sees approval in their wholesale tolerance of this dangerous nonsense.

His sense of values must change in the face of this vicious propaganda machine, whose sole purpose is to sell more goods to people already over-laden. And if he retains any sense of proportion, the clever people on Madison Avenue are ready with psychologists specially trained to overcome his doubt and orient him towards their clients' products.

One cannot raise children in a climate of deceit without perverting their moral values. The child lives in two worlds. There is school where the climate is, hopefully, more in keeping with his true development. There the child absorbs some of the values necessary for his growth as a mature, selective adult of good taste. But outside school, the child is confronted by the advertisers intruding in all areas of his life. There is no follow-up on his teachers' attempts to shape his sense of values.

We are so used to "free" entertainment we hardly question the enormous price we ultimately pay. We absorb the mushy programs and advertising through our pores. It is the most costly thing we can buy. Those silken-voiced trustworthy men and women come into our living rooms daily and piously tell us to buy this and that, their demeanor that of the priest in the pulpit. Can they all be truthful? The child wonders and finally decides they are all liars. But where will he find the truth? His parents are the final judges of right and wrong, but they watch the false prophets of commerce without question.

There was a time when the only voice purring unctuously outside school was the voice of the church but that voice was, at least, selling God. Now the prophets speak all over the country, and their product is anything in a bottle or a wrapper that carries an advertising budget. Even some of the churches have copied the tactics of the pitchmen.

The radio and T.V. entertainment may be free, but the price we pay for it is the erosion of the growth, taste and character of our young.

We complain that we don't understand teenagers, and they don't understand us. We blame the teenager for his cynicism, his lack of trust and his refusal to communicate. Is he at fault? He is not the author of his environment; he has had good teachers — us. If his moral code is slack, he's had good examples — us. If he's indifferent to anyone but himself, we have shown the way. Since babyhood he has seen us worshipping the Golden Calf. His childhood is one long memory of our obsession with money, the love of it, the need of it, the lack of it. The richest nation in the world has more people constantly needing more money than any other country. The richest nation in goods and services has more people coveting possessions than any other nation. Throughout his life at home the child sees his parents' happiness constantly dependent on more money, a bigger house, new clothing and a new car. All happiness stems from buying. We have forgotten that our real happiness can only come from within, from non-material things like love, contact, and through our growth as integral parts of our environment.

To illustrate further how totally indifferent we have become, we accepted a gross situation a few years ago and never even commented upon it. An American President became a national salesman! We had had a slight recession. People began saving instead of buying and some people got their spending in tune with their earnings for the first time in years. Unemployment began to rise, the stock market began to fall. The President came on the air. "You ought to buy — buy — buy — buy! Buy till it hurts, don't save — buy!" The recession slowed and stopped. Merchants began to increase their inventories. Manufacturers began to stockpile; a newly thrifty people took their money out of their savings and began to buy those anxiously needed goods. The stock market rose and unemployment fell off. And — the children and the teenagers sat back and stared — then fell on each others necks and howled in disbelief. For now the Great White Father — the Chief — the man upstairs had spoken and not only had he blessed this indulgence, he actually commanded it! The recession might have been averted in other ways; previous recessions have, but now the panic button was pressed in a way the kids would not forget.

There is another situation, not readily understood by parents, which has serious repercussions on the young. Every child is really, in terms of his own money, a poor relation, an under-privileged person. Ignorant of long-range goals that might help him mature as an adult with proportion and perspective, he looks to his parents for the proper examples. He comes into the world naked; he has nothing. He soon learns about possessions in the shape of toys and other extravagant gifts his guilty parents shower on him. He rarely gets the chance to develop love for one particular toy and the pleasure of making the inanimate object part of him through use and affection. Toys of every description and complication come pouring down on him like an avalanche. He stands, hands upstretched with a grin of stupifying pleasure and cries: "More, more!" And the more he desires, the greater his need. He quickly learns from his parents that money is the key to more possessions and the need of possessions grows in him like a sickness.

Like his parents he never has enough. But his parents have money, the means of satisfying their desires. For him, there is another way — stealing. And his parents can't figure out why this child, coming from a good home, having everything he wanted — should steal.

By the time he reaches mid-teens it is cars and other unearned possessions. Many parents try to buy their children's love with gifts and are confounded by the absence of gratitude. The parents create in the child an artificial, insatiable want, which does not produce gratitude, only desire. Trained young in a false sense of values by uninspired parents, greedy merchants and lying advertisers, here are our consumers of the future.

In the mad scramble for sexual equality many women have interpreted social equality as emasculation and competition with men. Unfortunately, many men aid and abet this suicidal endeavor resulting in the emergence of a masculine-oriented womanhood, strident, domineering and aggressive. On the other hand, males have lost much of their manliness, strength and leadership. Mama is boss. And she has advertisers, insurance companies, and the politicians to prove it. Mama is the one who stands behind Dad and puts the backbone into him. Mama is the leader, except in the supermarket where she follows Dad out to the parking lot — Dad is, of course, pushing the market cart. Mother is dominant and sensible, Dad can't make up his mind. These are the examples our children observe. Who is the male, who is the female? Will the daughter pattern herself after the female who acts like a man, or after the male who acts like a woman? Who will the son follow?

There appears to be reluctance on the part of woman to behave like women. To be feminine and submissive is equated with weakness — to expose oneself to be used and trod upon. By the same token there is a reluctance among men to be masculine, aggressive and strong. Somehow these male characteristics are equated with toughness and bullying. Yet millions of American women daily fantasize about an aggressive male. Witness the success of "Gone With The Wind" and the longings of American womanhood who wished they could stand-in for Scarlet O'Hara when she got thrown on the bed without so much as a by-your-leave by Rhett Butler.

A woman can't be happy unless she feels like a woman, and makes femininity and gentleness her strength. This softness in the female produces hardness in the male — in the organ where it counts the most! We call ourselves the greatest nation in the world and yet this simple truth escapes us. There is nothing like a woman to make a man feel truly a man — and nothing like a man to make a woman feel truly like a woman.

So the female emulates the man and wonders why she is not loved, and the male emulates the female and wonders why his wife fails to give him an erection. — I am becoming more and more convinced that the penis is the most intelligent part of the male body. I am sure that nature vested in this organ instincts that transcend our over-developed head culture. Faced with challenge and domination by the female, it shrinks, recoils, — but rises forth gallantly in salutation to the submissive female whom nature really had in mind for this tribute. It is good for the male to be hard and forceful and for the female to be soft and yielding. But when personalities do not follow this pattern then our sexual pattern is likely to follow our personal deficiencies.

Into this sorry state our young are raised. Children need both a strong parent and a gentle one. Who is who? The boy can't use Dad as his hero — he's too weak. He dare not follow mother — she's too strong — so he fashions a neutral makeshift role for himself which later produces horrendous personality problems.

On whom does daughter pattern herself, feminine father or masculine mother ? The pattern set by the strong mother and the weak father become the archetypes of a new generation.

Parents cannot comprehend the stark chill in the child's mind at the time of divorce. For them there is some compensation. The wife hopes to find a new, more loving mate. The man feels the misery of divorce will be balanced by the departure of an unloving wife. But for the child there is no compensation. It is soul shattering, and it is, forever! It is a calamity his mind cannot grasp and its refusal to accept this tragedy creates further problems. It is necessary for growth that we acknowledge the many changes inevitable in life; that we accept them mentally and emotionally. By so doing we are able to function and grow. These adjustments are difficult for most adults to make and to comprehend. How, therefore, do we expect a child to accept emotionally so huge a change, that is not of his making, and one that defies adults many years his senior to accept?

In his confusion he must have permanence, he must be able to rely on people and ideals; without them he is lost. His mother and father *must* go on for him — forever. For him to accept the fact they can divorce, go their separate ways, become strangers, is to deny his own existence. There is a family, a finality. He is his father's son, his mother's boy — his heart tells him this. If this is not true, then who is he? If mother and father can become strangers, what chance is there for dependence on anything.

So life plays its cruelest tricks upon the child. And although he does not accept this mad situation, an ideal begins to erode and is replaced by a withdrawal and skepticism. This is nature's adjustment. It enables him to go on. He will pay heavily later as an adult for this survival technique.

It is said, hopefully and foolishly, that a child is better off in a divorce situation than living with parents who don't love each other and who quarrel. Not true! The child is better off with both parents, who may perhaps learn there are other methods than divorce. It may involve giving something of themselves, of making an effort to consider the other partner. If they do not learn this they will have to in a future marriage — or — end up alone forever.

Parents who adopt this frivolous attitude have long forgotten their own childhood. In himself the child has little security or strength. His world had definite though limited boundaries of security, and the cornerstones are mother and father. It is no more lasting than they are lasting. What is his situation then if they break up — change their status from father and mother to that of strangers? Add to this appalling circumstance, the state of his mind when those loved ones become angry, bitter foes. He sees his home and family dissolved, a disaster he can no more comprehend than his own dissolution. And these loved ones are tearing at each other like wild beasts. I do not say that the conditions that create an unhappy marriage must be sustained for the sake of the children but divorce is not the only alternative. There is another way, that is, to use the strength and character of both partners to overcome the trials that are almost inevitable in any marriage. Such an achievement keeps the child with his natural parents, solves the male — female dilemma and advances human spiritual growth. It strengthens the character of those who face this difficult task with courage and determination, so that each successive trial is more easily overcome until eventually marital problems all but disappear.

Perhaps it is too much to expect married couples to understand that character and strength are not developed by good times, but in how we meet and overcome the bad ones; that we do not grow as adults in warm breezes, but in how we handle the storms.

But, we are a "fun" nation. And marriage must be fun or it is a mistake. Our obsession with fun is so great that we go to enormous lengths to avoid challenges. Children quickly learn this fun habit from their parents. School, for the most part, becomes not life's first hurdle, but a fun place too. Students and parents measure school successes in terms of social acceptance and popularity.

In most European countries, the aim of education is character building and the development of future responsible citizens. Application to study is serious and requirements high. Diplomas are issued not for attendance but for achievement. We view European education with some distaste; it's too demanding, too serious.

We have a great ambition: Education is for EVERYBODY. This is a noble and worthy thought. But then we go on to say: "Everybody *must* be educated."

In "The Prophet" by Gibran, the prophet is asked: "And what of Education?" He answers: "The teacher must bring the student to the portals of the temple, but the student must enter by himself." We bring the student to the temple, we carry him through the doors and drag him down the nave.

There are very few things which can be mass produced and still contain beauty and uniqueness let alone quality. And mass-produced education is no exception. The result: prefabricated adults, ready to fly apart when unusual strains are put upon them.

Our educational system has taken a 180-degree turn from the British system and overcompensated to the extent that we have overmatched their weaknesses. In pre-war Britain's elementary schools the academic testing time came at the ripe old age of eleven. Children were given the supreme test of their educational career, known as the Junior County Scholarship Exam. This exam was deliberately designed to eject close to ninety percent of students from school at age 14; a scant ten per cent passed and qualified for secondary school. Hence, Britain was able to build a large army of workers with just enough equipment to read and write. In the United States we go whole hog in the other direction, and everybody is considered high school material. Somebody said: "Everyone should have a high school diploma," So we try to give every student the means to obtain this coveted certificate. But opportunity is only one of the essentials which makes a scholar. He must have drive, ambition and a personal need for higher education. And, if the desire for more schooling has not crystallized in a student at the age of 15 or 16, it is absurd to push him forward against his inclinations.

The results of this folly are evident all around us. We have the widest educational system in the world — and the thinnest. The child without aptitude or desire dilutes the quality of the system as a whole thus robbing the youngster with drive and ability. Higher education should be at the disposal of all children subject to a test at age 15 or 16. The assessment at this time of desire and aptitude should be the criterion for further schooling, rather than the present system which depends upon the candidate's ability to score minimal passing grades. It is ludicrous to see young men and women plodding daily to school when they have no interest in academic pursuits; who find themselves unwilling participants in what must seem to them a juvenile exercise.

There are hundreds of thousands of young men who would be more useful to themselves and society in other occupations.

They would be happier and more productive working in a man's world, with men's rules.

This compulsory higher education, coupled with employers' insistence that applicants for jobs must have high school diplomas or degrees, is as much a penalty as the late 19th century enforced labor of the young. Teenagers have their own special ways of dealing with this unrealistic imposition, — gangs, fighting, stealing and delinquency. Try telling a 6'2" boy of 16 weighing 200 lbs that he is going to be punished for a school rule infraction.

Many of these young men would become responsible adults if they went to work. There they would be disciplined by men; they would learn to abide by men's rules. There would be no contempt for the instructor, for the punishment would be of a different caliber, the scorn of older men, the loss of a job and earning power.

This wiser economic use of young men with no interest in further education would give the dedicated student a better opportunity to develop his potential in a less-crowded school. And, incidentally, drastically reduce local taxes.

Another aspect of our school system which prevents it from functioning as an important area of guidance and character development, is the traditional American horror of discipline. Even though we have great need for much regulation in this direction, we go to enormous lengths to reduce whatever authority schools and teachers may have. So much of the children's home life reflects a lack of concern on his parents' part that his need for definite guidelines is even stronger in school. Yet our system is such that we carry all the weakness and disorder of our homes into the school. This is manifested by the two agencies which destroy the purpose of the school and the efficiency of the teacher. Namely, the non-scholastic, political school board, and the P.T.A.

We don't trust the school and the teacher. Actually, we have a profound distrust of intellectuals — eggheads, and even education! It is assumed that the teacher is the right person for the job of teacher. I don't believe there is any other job in the

world where the efforts of professionals are so seriously
hamstrung by the subjective opinions of novices as in the
schools' operation. We intrude in a mass and confound the
results that could best be obtained by teachers. Why anybody
imagines teachers must subject themselves to such an ill-
informed body as the P.T.A., whose only claim to scholastic
distinction is procreative ability, is beyond my comprehension.

Would we dare organize a P.S.A. — a Parents-Science-
Association; a P.D.A. — a Parents-Diplomats-Association, to
discuss relations with other nations? Would we organize a
P.P.A. — a Parents' Pilots Association to assist running the
airlines? Why, therefore, thrust our ill-informed opinions upon a
body of highly trained specialists who perform one of the most
important jobs in the country, the teaching of our children?

The teacher cannot be effective. He is rendered impotent by
students bigger than he. He is curbed by politicians who may
find his philosophy and ideas offensive. He is chastened by the
political trend of the day and must adjust truth because his ideas
are not currently popular. And, finally, he is subjected to the
scrutiny of laymen who qualify for membership in the local
P.T.A.

One more note on public school life. I have never felt that
coeducation was the best method of achieving scholastic ability.
As a means of vying for popularity it is hard to beat, but I do
not see how greater concentration on studies can be ac-
complished when so much energy and interest must automatically be drawn towards members of the opposite sex. The
lengths teenagers go to, to be sexually provocative, must inevitably bend the mind towards more exciting adventures than
study. Perhaps we adults have forgotten the overwhelming
sexual drives of our own teens. Certainly America's classrooms
stimulate and provoke an already aroused youth — but not in
the direction of higher learning.

It is necessary to instill pride and self-respect in the young. It
must be astonishing for visitors from poor countries who see the
unkempt, shabby appearance of typical junior and high school
students. Dirty shoes, ragged blue jeans and old sweaters.

"Why?" they ask. The answer invariably is, "There is no point in giving them good clothes, they'll only dirty and tear them." In most European countries, children of families with very low incomes attend school decently dressed and groomed. Orderly dress is not the result of wealth or snobbishness, but serves a more valuable purpose. It is recognized that pride in clothes and appearance has an important influence on behavior. Dress sloppily and we eliminate pride in deportment. The value of good grooming is recognized in all walks of life — except in school. There, young ladies dress with the accent on seduction and social popularity, and young men, as though they were going camping.

One more aspect of our national life and its influence on the young passes unnoticed in our search for the "good life": the quadrennial American electioneering ritual with its copious usage of clichés, snake-oil polemics and boasting.

In retrospect, these exercises are amusing. Such long, windy speeches, such devotion to A-M-E-R-I-C-A and Godliness. Such blasts and noise leading up to the primaries and general elections. And then suddenly there's silence . . . not a whisper. The noise and shouting is over. The silence is as intense as the noise was loud. It was as though Rip Van Winkle emerged from his long sleep, took hurried stock of his country's health, stormed and ranted, and then returned to the deep well of sleep from whence he came.

Special courses must be taken to teach otherwise intelligent men how to deliver speeches that consist mainly of platitudes, bull-shit and motherhood.

Every four years the country is in imminent danger of collapse and ruin. We are informed we are on the road to moral decay. We are governed, we are told, by liars, hypocrites, semi-dictators, neo-fascists and communists. We are warned of corruption, theft and patronage in high office. The President and his cabinet are depicted as crooks, weaklings and idiots. And we also have the spectacle of members of the same party hurling insults and wild charges at each other in the primaries.

All this hullabaloo, blown up with the aid of millions of dollars, PR men, press, radio and TV when viewed through the sobering light 21 days after the elections, reveals what a public travesty and lot of nonsense it surely is. For three years this country lives and runs its normal course quietly and peacefully through good times and bad with problems met and crises overcome. Then, at the beginning of the fourth, a rumbling is heard which develops by stages into an ear-splitting roar, with an ever-increasing intensity as the year climaxes. If the dangers to the country were real during the election, they must be real after the election. If we are governed by idiots and crooks prior to the election, we are governed by idiots and crooks after the election. If sincerity and love of country compel our candidates to utter these warnings, why are they so silent later?

Are these circuses, the conventions, with grown-up men and women armed with noise makers and funny hats, milling and churning around and cheering to the impassioned pleas for the A-M-E-R-I-C-A-N WAY OF LIFE and motherhood, necessary for the election of an American President? When your young view these scenes on the TV and try to reconcile the importance of America on the world stage, the age of atomic and hydrogen bombs and flights to the moon, they must have difficulty in remembering these are America's most important men and women and not a convention of toy manufacturers.

These lunatic spectacles belong a hundred years ago, safely concealed by a pre-radio and TV era. But the need to advertise candidates in the media is more important to the political parties than the destructiveness such shallowness and insincerity has upon the minds of the young.

The American people are grossly underestimated and shamelessly abused by the antics of political parties at election time. Do the politicians seriously believe they have to give the public a three-ring carnival to make the people listen and vote. Whoever underrated the American electorate so poorly as to imagine that it must be subjected to such hypocrisy before it reacts? Who said one must find a weakness in one's opponent and blast away in order to win votes? Who claimed the public is so gullible to fall for the wild muck-raking and smearing made by so-called dignified candidates for public office? Who said you have to repeat the same nonsense every day, all day, for a whole year before the public gets the message?

It is revolting to listen to the unashamed, brazen use of platitudes and the flagrant appeals to emotionalism made by candidates. The American public deserves better.

What do other countries think of us when they hear candidates for the presidency call each other liars? What is the effect of this ugliness upon our young and impressionable teenagers? They do read newspapers and listen to radio and TV. Do they become cynical and disbelieve this nonsense? That is quite a price to pay. Cynicism instead of admiration.

Our politicians treat us as though we have the mentality of peasants. They appeal to the basest emotionalism of the lowest intelligence.

But the young are listening. They are still able to look up and admire the heroes of the country. Will they find them among the presidential nominees?

Parents sometimes take trouble to shield their kids from family quarrels. Why bother when the children can look in and witness the gigantic dog fights of elections?

Morality is preached, shouted boomed and repeated by candidates until one feels one is witnessing the world's greatest revival meeting. But the kids equate Christianity with morality. In church these words mean one thing, in the elections another. Does it matter if we destroy their faith as long as we win elections?

Where in this country will the child find his true standards of morality and values? In the home tottering on the brink of divorce — father and mother vilifying each other? In the schools, mass produced and bowing to expediency? In the money grubbing "sell at any cost" world of our culture? On the radio and TV with the low pap entertainment and the commercials screaming incessantly? In the wide country of America where the candidates for public office scream, distort, confuse and accuse each other with all the venom of fish-wives, the tub-thumping of hucksters and the psychotic evangelism of Elmer Gantry?

Don't let the young drive before a certain age. Don't let them go into bars before they are twenty-one. Remove dirty books from magazine racks, and watch carefully what they are taught in school. But, by all means let them listen to all the screaming and yelling by men who are supposed to be the most eminent in the country.

The average child can read at seven or eight. The average high school student is very much aware of the world about him. What lunacy then to present our future citizens with such disgusting spectacles during the most important chapter in our national life.

Who do the young look up to now? You can't get much higher than presidential candidates.

We should have large banners and posters displayed all over the land at election time warning bellicose politicians — "DON'T SCREAM OR SHOUT — THE CHILDREN MAY BE LISTENING!"

Conception does not automatically invest the female with wisdom, responsibility and an understanding of a child's needs — although our laws and courts hold steadfast to the notion that it does!

Chapter 11

CUSTODY...
A MATTER OF GENDER?

Earlier in this book, I suggested that many of our present laws and customs would be better suited to a bygone era when women played a far different role and deserved a greater protection by society. Heedless of social changes and 60 years too late, we now rush in willy-nilly to redress the ills of yesterday.

The effect of this misplaced zeal is to reverse the pendulum and so create an equal and opposite measure of social injustice. Society passively accepts this folly. Politicians dare not propose effective new laws; it would cost too many votes. The judiciary is too subservient or lethargic to propose such changes — no matter how long overdue.

With respect to the custody of children, we pattern our laws not on common sense and reality but on a myth, a long-forgotten ideal.

It is inevitable in a divorce action, that the mother will get the children regardless of whether or not she has the native ability and the desire to be a mother and a homemaker. And regardless of whether the marriage break-up was due to her infidelity or even whim.

To automatically give the mother custody of the children without thoroughly assessing the worthiness and domestic responsibility of either parent, is to subscribe to a mechanical rote which makes a travesty of justice, a mockery of the courts and prepares the foundation for a possible blighted future for the children.

Of course, the children should stay with the mother — if indeed she is a mother in the true, and not just the biological sense of the word. For, in that capacity, she is the best suited parent to raise the child.

But this is an ideal. This might have been true years ago. But the training and evolution of women in the last 60 years has swept this concept aside. Conception and childbearing do not automatically invest the female with wisdom, responsibility and an understanding of a child's needs although laws and institutions hold steadfast to the notion that it does. A wife would have to be a whore for the husband to get custody and then the issue would be doubtful.

The situation in the early part of this century when women wanted to acquire the skills needed to run a home and desired the responsibility of a family while men had no such ambitions, has reversed. Today most women train for a job, career or profession outside the home. The knowledge of homemaking does not fall like a magic mantle on the shoulders of a woman once marriage and conception takes place.

Many women, ill-trained for marriage, do, in fact, feel frustrated and imprisoned when the romance of courtship is replaced by the reality of marriage and children. They envy their husbands and look to escape the narrow confines of domesticity by going out to work, returning home at night like any other wage earner. Their children are palmed off by these part-time mothers, on maids, grandmothers, or anyone who will have them.

I am not talking about all women. Some mothers are tender, warm, devoted and caring. But such mothers are not typical.

By the same token there are many fathers who hardly deserve the name. They ignore their responsibilities and are determined to satisfy their own desires regardless of the cost and heartache to wives and children — it would be just as criminal and immoral to give custody to such fathers simply because they have the ability to sire a child.

The purpose of child custody laws, theoretically, is to seek the best interests of the child. The courts claim they desire to protect the innocent victims of divorce. But the law is lazy and pays only lip service to its purpose. If it were not so, it would sift, weigh, analyze and investigate each separate case to find who, indeed, is the fit parent for custody. Instead it falls back on the outworn, unproven cliché that custody is a matter of gender — female gender, that is.

There are many instances where the child would be better off with his father — when the father is more oriented toward the security the child needs — home, continuity and love.

The law defeats its purpose. Many women do not wish to make a home in all that this term implies. Even though these women demand custody, they insist upon the freedom inherent in the single childless state. So, the father, deprived of the children he loves, loses them — not to his ex-wife, but to her parents or maid.

How can the courts claim to have the child's welfare at heart when, all too often, the child is doomed to have neither parent. No grandparent, baby-sitter or housekeeper could ever substitute for a father who is anxious to be a parent.

This is not to say that custody should automatically be given to the father — no more than to the mother. But rather, the background, maturity, goals and ambitions of both parents should be judged to determine who is the more suitable.

The myth that the courts are interested only in the welfare of the child is a cliché that would never stand up to any reasonable test. The courts provide a simplistic and dangerous answer because it is the easy way out. Our future citizens have their lives determined by short-sighted platitudinous judges. The number of children from broken homes account for an enormous part of the child population in California, and many of these children are with the wrong parent.

Astonishing though it may sound, there are probably more fathers today better suited to raise their children than their ex-wives. Men haven't changed too much in the last fifty years, except to possibly become more feminine. They still follow the historic pattern of male parenthood — the provider of the family's living and future.

Women, on the other hand, have rebelled and succeeded in breaking away from their natural roles. Adrift, midstream, they are not capable or inclined to the wife-mother function, nor are they successful in the male-father realm. They seem to flounder somewhere between. Therefore, of the two parents, the male still accepts and possesses the instinct and desires to be a father — a provider that has had thousands of years invested in its making, and around which society builds its very foundation.

The more the male strives to succeed in his work, the more he gains in his gender. Conversely, the more the female attempts to succeed in her new direction, the more she must lose in her gender. Her female instincts of motherhood, responsibility and automatic responsiveness to her children become atrophied when her energies are directed towards work and career.

Many women complain that they have so many problems with their children — the housekeeper can't seem to cope with them. In fact, housekeepers have to be changed frequently. If you get one who cooks, she can't clean. If she cleans, she's no good with the kids.

One woman I know, divorced three years, complained that her children were impossible. How much time did she spend with them, I asked. At least three evenings a week, she said, but she was tired after working, and had dates on other nights. Why did she entrust the maid with the important job of raising her children? She needed to work, she replied, to earn extra money — this in spite of alimony and child support.

The fact was that by the time she paid for the housekeeper and the uneconomical, inefficient way in which her home was run, she barely broke even. She didn't go to work to earn needed money, but to get away from her children — to avoid being a homemaker.

Why did the judge award the children to this mother? He should have given them to the housekeeper.

Mothers fight and plead to keep their children as their inalienable right, then having obtained custody, pass that responsibility along to someone else. Why do women so strenuously demand a responsibility they have no intention of meeting? Is it because it is fashionable and carries with it an important, but unearned status — or do they fear they will be stigmatized if they lose custody to the father?

Another possibility is the children can always be used as an ever-ready pipeline to the ex-husband's guilt, and purse. He will never get away from his ex-wife as long as she has the kids and he certainly doesn't want his own children to do without the good things in life.

We have come a long way from a meaningful life style when women prefer the dubious satisfactions of going to work to the fulfillment of raising one's own children and seeing them grow. It is not a simple task caring for a child, nor does it require a college degree, but the child does need a few basic fundamentals, love, continuity, the security of your presence, your firmness and dependability. With our working divorcee, the housekeeper fills in for mother, TV substitutes for love and guidance, and expedience supplants integrity. The child dare not become too attached to the housekeeper — she may leave one day, as did father, as does mother, daily. Attention is cursory, mother is always rushing off to work, is tired at night and sleeps late on weekends. The maid of course, is too busy running the house and taking care of Mommy (Mommy needs a Mommy) to give much attention to the kids.

Whom do the kids sit down with at breakfast and lunch? Security is fleeting, warmth a matter of guilt and firmness always absent. No maid has the ability and patience to cope with another woman's children.

How then would the father make a better custodial parent? Strange as it seems, more fathers enjoy their homes than do their ex-wives. The home provides him with a rest haven and a counterbalance to the pressures of the day's work. In fact, men require a similar environment as their children.

If both divorced parents work, then the ex-husband could well be a better choice for custody. He will be home more often with his children. Nor will he be as frustrated in his job or business as his ex-wife, since it is his natural role.

There is another factor which drastically reduces the effectiveness of the female as the children's guardian. Fearful that time is passing, she's forever on the search for another male. The fear of being left on the shelf drives her to spend more of her time hunting than her ex-husband — and for good reason. At 30, 40 or 50 a man is always a potential "catch," but with our divorced mother, 30 to 40, her field is narrowing rapidly. So, while the ex-husband is delighted to come home nights to his kids and be with them evenings, weekends and holidays, the mother plans her spare time with one eye always cocked for an eligible male.

Divorced mothers are not unmindful that men avoid women with children. Consequently, many of them assume the life style of a single woman without ties. This of course, places extra burdens on the maid, who extracts extra payment, in kind, in her attitude to the home and children.

When a working mother hires a maid, she is really hiring a surrogate mother, not for her children, but for herself. The limitation of the maid will eventually be reflected in the development of the children.

If, on the other hand, a divorced father hires a housekeeper, he will engage her with the children as his sole consideration. He will apply his business acumen to the selection of the most capable person available. Nor will he want the housekeeper to be his maid or his mother. He is not running from his natural vocation to an unnatural one. He is still performing his regular parental function as a breadwinner and father. The care and responsibility of the children imposes no extra strain on him. On the contrary, they give his life meaning and substance.

Loudly and clearly, it must be said, the concerned divorced father knows a thousand times better than a rubber stamp judge what is best for his own children. He should remind the judge that in time of war his country urges him to go out and fight, to protect his home and family from the enemy. He complies, is often wounded or killed. But the enemy is here, right in his own country, destroying his home and taking his children away. Men lose by default. It is their weakness in marriage which ends the contract. And it is this weakness in divorce which dooms the children with the wrong parent.

Customs evolve into laws, and laws create customs. Customs and laws change but not always when the need arises. There are many laws on our statute books and social customs which had meaning in the past but which are ludicrous and destructive today.

But how can such changes be brought about when so many men are passive and defeated before they begin. When the subject of custody comes up, the husband's attorney invariably shrugs and says: "We don't stand a chance." Bunk! If a father is willing to fight for his child and can prove he is a better parent, that the welfare of the child will suffer if it remains with the mother, I cannot believe the court will abandon justice and deny custody to the party presenting the worthier case.

It is not often done; there are few strong fathers. So few, in fact, that on the rare occasion when a father contests the issue of custody, it makes the newspapers.

Earlier I stated that one of the father's prime roles in parenthood is to help the child separate — to grow into a self-sufficient human being. Frequently, even in a happy home, the mother will resist the tug as her "baby" grows away from her. It is a difficult time for a woman, but with the father's presence and love, she accepts this healthy evolution of the child.

The tragedy of divorce and the tunnel-vision of the courts spells the end of the father's participation in the child separating process. The mother is a bad substitute. She frequently retards and damages the child's outward journey by laying on him trips of guilt through her dread of the day he will leave her.

In her loneliness, she turns to the child for the satisfaction of needs which can never be satisfied. With a son, she molds him into a sort of husband-by-proxy; with a daughter, into a guilt-

ridden minion for life. Such children will always be dependent
and tied to mother. They may never marry and if they do the
chances of them becoming mature husbands, wives and parents
are remote. Every time the son tries to separate, his guilt will
engulf him. He will be torn between hatred of his mother (more
guilt) and hatred of himself. Constant will be his ever-present
need to see and call her, to see if she is all right. She will never
be all right. She embarked upon a course which defies nature
and which, if practiced in the animal world, would lead to its
destruction.

In such circumstances many a father would be a healthier and
more suitable parent for his children. Men are happy and feel
fulfilled when they see their children separating, emerging and
developing the skills needed for their future lives.

The problem is almost insoluble. Regardless of how a man
meets the divorce situation his interests and those of his children
are going to be badly served. In this dilemma the father can
adopt one of two attitudes. He can take whatever crumbs the
courts and his wife allow him and play a vague and shadowy
role as a part-time father, or he can try and cut himself off from
any feelings toward his children.

Some men follow the latter course, and are bitterly condemned by wives, who want to have their cake and eat it too —
and by society. It is sad to see the way children of divorced
parents reach out hungrily for a male, any male. When the
mother's new date calls for her the eyes of the kids widen and
hopefully latch on to this new male.

But one wonders if that apparently indifferent man who was
their father is entirely wrong. No matter what he does, the
solution, barring one avenue, custody, is going to be intolerable
and unbearably painful. Cutting communication at least numbs
the hurt.

There are horrors galore awaiting the divorced father who is
deprived of his children. I am sure most men would never marry
if they could foresee the shape of things to come.

The father whose feelings for his children remain strong and
sensitive, in spite of divorce, exposes himself to a hurt that has

no parallel in any other sphere of life. An inevitable recurring pain that he can do nothing about.

In the limited area left to him after divorce, the father becomes a shadow who emerges once or twice a month. He is expected to pick up the pieces and create a new life for himself, yet he must remain a silent and impotent witness to anything that may occur as a consequence of his children's environment.

Concerned and alarmed by positive manifestations of problems emerging in his children, four courses of action are available to the troubled father, all of them tortuous and destructive.

DISCUSSING THE CHILDREN'S PROBLEMS WITH HIS EX-WIFE:

Woe betide him if he embarks upon this adventure. His manner of address may be gentle, and tactful but immediately the children's mother bristles. Any suggestion on his part, no matter how reasonable and carefully couched, is viewed as an intrusion into her exclusive domain and an attack on her person and ability. Her response to the slightest suggestion that she might be making some mistakes in the manner in which she is raising the children destroys all chances of reasonable dialogue and replaces the husband's original mission with a shooting match, a shooting match wherein the welfare of the children is forgotten. All suggestions are seen by her as insulting criticisms and declarations of unworthiness as mother, female and citizen.

To be sensitive and responsive to one's children and yet be powerless to intervene when the occasion warrants, is a ghastly prospect, an ongoing condemnation to hell.

The father may have visiting rights, but decisions affecting the children are not equally divided, no matter what was decreed in court. Mother is the supreme arbiter, and he, the father, is reduced to the status of an uncle — a distant relative. The wife now considers the children her sole property. Her decisions, for good or for bad and her authority are exclusive and final. She regards her ex-husband as completely outside the area of advice and decision, an interloper.

How does the wife get this idea? Through a sort of divine right of motherhood? Perhaps she derives this concept from the judge's bias, during the divorce hearing. This is all well and good when the mother is mature, loving and responsive to her children's needs. But, even then, the father can still play a valuable part in helping to raise them. Unfortunately, when the courts award custody to the mother they do not award wisdom at the same time.

FATHER ATTEMPTS TO NEUTRALIZE PROBLEMS ON VISITING DAYS:

As an alternative to the hopeless task of discussing the children's problems with their mother, this avenue is even more futile and harmful to the children. The father's time with his children is limited and any gains he might achieve are swiftly erased when the children return to their mother. Continued efforts by him create a never-ending battle, a tug of-war, with the children always the rope. Confusion and a lowered sense of confidence develops in the children as they are torn in two directions. This bewilderment becomes even more seriously compounded as the kids, fearful of losing the love of either parent, try to please both. This impossible compromise guarantees the future onset of neurosis. In their attempt to be all things to opposing parents, they become nothing in themselves — vague, indecisive non-persons.

In this battle, objectivity is lost, and the children become the front-line in the growing war. Matters affecting the children are seized upon as excuses by beleaguered parents to vent their spleen and spite on each other.

Should the father retain his sense of objectivity, his limited time with his children completely discourages him from enforcing previously inculcated precepts or — imposing further restraints and firmness. How can he? The kids will be returning to their mother at six o'clock and will be gone for two weeks. He doesn't want to play the heavy and he doesn't want them to take home unpleasant memories of him.

So when they deliberately ignore his request to turn off the TV and wash their hands before dinner, he can look away when they tune him out or endlessly repeat his instructions. The kids become clever at not hearing the Do's and Don'ts. They practice all day long with the maid. She, for her part, learned long ago that the kids are tougher than she, and her job doesn't pay enough to compensate for such a brutal task.

So Dad becomes a passive, weak pushover — or a crippling nag, qualities not destined to aid the children along the road to healthy growth.

DEADLOCK WITH EX-WIFE. FATHER DECIDES TO ENGAGE A LAWYER AND TAKE HER TO COURT:

This last is a real lulu! This is the much-vaunted course pre-scribed by the courts as proof positive of equity for all under the law. However, having been passive during marriage, divorce and custody, men are not now about to emerge as giants in this more intense drama. The emotions flare up with greater volatility than at any other time. Lawyers and *adversary* strategies again enter the picture. Memories are painfully wracked to try to separate fact from emotion. Passions flood and spill over, for now the children, the fruit of their union are also the seeds of the parents' discord. Accusations and counter-accusations are anticipated and mentally answered. The brain seethes. "All the other things I haven't thought of yet." Health suffers, costs mount.

Mother enters the courtroom serene and convinced she can do no wrong. She has never done anything wrong! With years of tradition behind this assurance and with the confident support of her attorney, she views this intruder in her private affairs — the children's father — as a second-class citizen. How dare he impugn the methods of Her Imperial Majesty? She stands always ready to shed a tear for the sympathetic and very busy judge, whose own mother undoubtedly implanted within him the conviction that *mothers can do no wrong.*

We can well imagine the effect the employment of this "equitable system of justice" is going to have upon the children.
. . . And what if the father should go to court this time? Is this the pattern for him and the children for the next ten years every time his ex-wife refuses to discuss a problem affecting the children . . . in and out of court?

In our great democracy this is definitely a rich man's enterprise. The law of equality does not operate here. The average citizen can find himself broke after one of these encounters and, since we live in a money culture, the possibilities of happiness in a future marriage can be seriously jeopardized.

It must be patently clear by now that the courts do not have the child's best interest at heart — they actually promote the child's **worst** interests.

The courts are much too busy to investigate, carefully weigh and analyze the true picture during a divorce action, it is said. The courts are piling up cases faster than they can be handled.

This is nonsense and a bankrupt attitude. It is precisely because they don't spend time in diligent investigation during divorce actions that they have such limited time. Their mass-produced methods of dealing with the greatest problem in this country is contributing mightily to the ever-increasing divorce rate and the consequent overcrowding of the courts.

In almost all enterprises involving the so-called mechanics of "saving time," the results generally reaped are an ever increasing shortage of time. The courts, wading swiftly through masses of divorces because they are overcrowded, make unwise decisions which in turn produce still more cases and still less time.

COMPLETE DISASSOCIATION OF THE FATHER FROM HIS CHILDREN.

In consideration of the three previous alternatives, this last might well be the best for all. Certainly, the father and the children are going to suffer less than in any of the former. To have to choose abandonment of your children as the only safeguard to your and their health is a damning indictment of judges and our perverted child custody laws. Through fitting himself into society's arbitrary mandate that custody is a matter of gender, the father has to cut himself off physically and emotionally from his children because this is the least damaging alternative offered by the courts.

Husbands do not comprehend at the time of divorce that when the judge awards the wife custody, he is, in essence, divorcing the children from their father.

It is said, with no little truth, that love is a matter of association. Once every week or two the father tries to maintain a bond with his children. He finds that the warm ties forged by daily contact are slipping away. He meets them under unnatural circumstances — often in his tiny furnished apartment, hardly a place where he and the children can be at ease in a home-like atmosphere.

Seeing them so seldom, he feels he needs to entertain them constantly. This imposes a strain on all of them. Out to the amusement park, the movies, beach or show. Out all the time. No home life together. There is less and less to talk about. He is on the outside.

So he spoils them, buys them things and hopes to buy their love. Everybody tries to buy their love. Mother, working and guilty, spoils them. Her boyfriends arrive with gifts for the kids.The grandparents shower them with money and toys; they are sorry for the poor little mites. Exit father, exit security and discipline.

Men have strange ways of resolving the divorce dilemma. A man who has lost his home and children is thrust against his wishes into bachelorhood. Mealtimes are casual excursions; the "fridge" contains only a few basic ingredients: a six pack of beer, old pre-cut cheese, a carton of two-week old milk and a bottle of champagne which has been in the ice-box for three months in the hope of an appreciative date. And — over everything, a liberal sprinkling of home-grown penicillin, that's been moldering in the "fridge" for months. No wonder he dashes the kids off to the beach or a show and then back home to their mother. This is the home he condemns himself to live in and play the part of father every second Sunday in the month from noon to 6 p.m.

It beats the hell out of me but it seems that every divorced man I know deliberately dons a hair shirt and condemns himself to live in some god-forsaken hole when he is evicted from his own home and hearth. These men select some moth-eaten furnished room or apartment of a much lower standard than they can actually afford. This sacrifice adds splendidly to their loneliness and despair and, by comparison, creates a false but beautiful image of their erstwhile comfortable "happy" home.

If there ever was a time in a man's life when he should indulge himself with a luxurious apartment, even if it is beyond his means, it is right now. He needs the moral boost of cheerful pleasant surroundings. He might not feel so much like a whipped cur that "no one loves."

If all the foregoing were the only experiences the father was going to encounter they would be bad enough, but there are still more ordeals harrowing enough to make him look enviously at the father who, at the time of the divorce, divorced himself from his children.

In these pages I have described many of the withholdings in marriage, the pain and cost of divorce, that awaits the future groom, but the biggest loss to the man is the loss of his children.

Since the mother is supposedly the maker of the nest she gets custody. She may also claim the right to work and that too is her right as an emancipated woman. Consequently she may choose to follow her career to another city or state, and that of course, is her right as a job holder. But all these contradictory judicial rights remove the children from their father forever.

At this stage, we have to conclude the female really has things going for her. The original theory behind female custody was that the man worked and the mother was the homemaker. But this is not the way it works out. Whenever the mother elects to work out of town the courts will agree that the children must go with her.

What happens now to the father who held on to his love for his children? Does he forget them or break his heart?

As opposed to the freedom and mobility of the female, the average man is more securely tied to one place, than the woman of yesterday ever was. A man's business, his monthly payments, alimony and child-support binds him more effectively to his own backyard than any bonds society could ever devise.

The woman, on the other hand, armed with child support, alimony, property settlement and hopes of a career, has nothing to hold her back. She can go anywhere to follow her "chosen work." And the courts smile benevolently and repeat: "The child should be with its mother." What mother? This kind of mother never put the child first. No roots hold her, no home binds her. She would as soon live in a hotel.

Yet the courts give her custody. She doesn't want to stay home. When she does find a home, the housekeeper will stay home, yet the courts give her custody. She has no intention of giving her children permanence or a sense of belonging to a community. Her own needs come first. Yet the courts give her custody. She hates housework, cooking and mending — yet the court gives her custody.

Just as a weak, indulgent parent can spoil a child and make a monster out of him, so too can a weak society, through its custom of rewarding delinquency, make a monster out of the parent.

The ex-wife may also marry a man who lives in another state. What happens to the kids? You guessed it! The courts pontificate: "The children should be with their mother." So buckle up, fathers-to-be, you have a lot of character building awaiting you. Try being a dad when your children are living 300 to 3,000 miles away.

There is an answer to this dilemma — if men would only see it. Two answers in fact.

ONE: Never marry; adopt your children — if this is not possible in this country, then adopt a couple of Tahitian or Korean babies. No woman, not even the one you eventually marry, unless you were fool enough to give her joint custody, could ever take them away from you.

TWO: Get a housekeeper, two if you like; it would still be cheaper than a wife, and you don't need a lawyer to fire her.

A child needs the presence of a male during marriage and it needs, even more, this male-father-strength after divorce.

There is a terrible inevitability about the problems awaiting the young married couple in America today. Sexual problems, adjustment problems, marital, divorce and custody problems and there is more than a 50 per cent chance they are going to fall heir to some or all of these horrors. Yet society beams and wish the couple well as though the act of marriage would automatically instill the knowledge, maturity and wisdom needed for its success. As though the ceremony would compensate for the lack of training and objectives and negate the vast accumulation of false values inherent in the couple's upbringing.

There is so much we have forgotten as a people in our blind rush into marriage, our automatic granting of divorce and custody and our automatic investment of the female with so much power and decision. We have turned our backs on the experience and tradition of the centuries in our slavish kowtowing to the distaff side.

We have forgotten that the father's greatest gift is not alimony or financial support but the experience, wisdom and strength acquired by him in his own lifetime, now hopefully to be passed on to his children. This is the only worthwhile gift he can endow. The real contribution of the father dies with him at divorce.

We spend over 100 billion dollars annually on defense. But what are we defending — our bankrupt way of life? This is as absurd as buying a battleship to safeguard the right of a leaking ship to sink. Our values and priorities are confused. Would it not be more profitable for the nation to spend its wealth, talent and ability in creating solvency first, so we have something to defend?

When the male begins to comprehend the enormous significance of the divorce laws, his embryonic manly nature takes a hurried and frightened departure. Realising that this wife may obtain a divorce on almost any grounds, he plays it safe and rarely opposes her.

Chapter 12

COMMUNITY PROPERTY — LICENSE TO STEAL

Mankind has fashioned many ennobling laws in the course of his long history. Conquered civilizations bequeathed to their victors customs and statutes developed during their growth and evolution.

The community property laws of California were inherited from Mexico, which, in turn, inherited them from Spain. Along with our adoption of California, we adopted these laws but, unfortunately, we did not retain the neutralizing body of Spanish law which served to offset their adverse effect.

The Spaniards developed the principle that the estate of the husband, developed during marriage, should be shared equally by the wife. But to counterbalance abuses which might arise through the vesting of so much power in the female, a canon of Catholic Spain forbade divorce and so canceled out any future division of the husband's estate. The Spanish wife looked upon her husband as her protector, bore him children and was happy and fulfilled in her domain, her home. Consequently, while she was an equal partner in the eyes of the law, she never exercised her rights since she never divorced her partner.

Ironically enough, her moral claim to a share in the community asset was greater than that of her American sister since she devoted her life not to a career, but to those more important areas of life which do not produce material wealth. Her right to a share in the estate was just, since the means of making a living for her and her children had traditionally been denied her.

Community property laws in California extend to rich and poor alike, but it is the middle, upper-middle and rich classes who feel the brunt of their inequities. We do not, of course, share Catholic Spain's prohibition of divorce. We actually have an opposite condition with wholesale and widespread divorce, with many people remarrying and divorcing several times over. When this antiquated law is not neutralized by the prohibition of divorce, injustice is inevitable.

Most divorce actions originate with wives. Frequently the grounds for the divorce are transparently trivial. Mental cruelty used to be the favorite. This excuse actually encourages women to take this drastic step. It promotes lack of restraint in many wives who know they will be rewarded handsomely if they abandon marriage — for abandonment it is.

Abandonment of an accepted responsibility in our society brings with it some form of punishment. In this most important of all contracts, the situation is reversed and rewards are substituted for punishment. Were all women mature, wise, responsible and dependable as far as their contractual obligations are concerned, there would be no fear of abuse. But such a state of affairs is wishful thinking and not related to the facts of life. Men differ greatly from women in this respect: when they marry they feel it will be for life. As a consequence, men invest most of their energies in the creation of a living for their families. In addition, many men devote their surplus energy to building an estate for the future security of their wives and children. This estate has value only as long as it remains undivided. This gift to his family is achieved by the husband working far beyond the call of duty, with more pressure than society expects of him.

Now, since the wife initiates the divorce action — with or without justification — this community asset must be divided. Two halves do not necessarily make a whole and, frequently, an estate which is divided ceases to exist. Many women, heedless of their husband's sacrifice, view this prize as a plum ripe for the plucking. Unfortunately, this arbitrary but legal exercise actually creates dire consequences for themselves and their children. Were it not for this attractive inducement to abandon marriage, many women might be encouraged to accept their roles and learn to overcome inevitable marital difficulties. Such a law does not promote social justice or fairness on either side. It creates bitterness in the man and a conviction that extra effort on behalf of his family is futile and even dangerous. It engenders discontent in the lonely divorcee who now holds the money bags in lieu of husband and marriage.

In spite of these laws, the average married American female is more discontented than her South American, Mexican, European and Japanese counterpart, who do not enjoy such legal protective devices. The law encourages the American female to take this financially rewarding but lonely step. In many cases the gain through community property division goes to pay for the upkeep of a current boyfriend or finance questionable business ventures which would make a banker blanch.

There is another destructive by-product of this absurd custom. In an age where many men find difficulty playing the male role, their difficulties are further compounded by so much power vested in the hands of the female.

Male-female relationships in our age are a source of never ending frustration. Women complain, (not without cause) of the lack of masculinity in men, and men bitch that women are no longer feminine and dependent.

It is not easy being a male in the U.S. His development is often stunted before its growth by the reversal of the male-female roles in his mother and father. Which is aggressive, which submissive? His lack of identification is further warped by his experience in elementary school. Instead of a male teacher, he is subject to female authority. When he does receive instruction from a man, much of its value is lost by the lack of respect and authority characteristic of our public school system. This authority is reduced further since teachers are held in low esteem because they do not meet our cultural definition of success — moneymaking.

By the time our young man arrives at marriage his nature has been badly tempered for the role he will play as husband and father. Problems will arise and his equipment will be badly strained meeting them. Unfortunately, the law now operates to cripple further any latent assertiveness and self-confidence he may develop replacing them with weakness.

When the male begins to comprehend the enormous significance of the divorce laws, his embryonic manly nature takes a hurried and frightened departure. Realizing that divorce may be obtained on any grounds, most men rarely oppose their wives.

"Mental cruelty" can be anything from putting your foot down as far as your wife's mother is concerned, to just plain standing up to your spouse. In the average marriage, a man risks the charge of "mental cruelty" several times a day. What a frightening prospect! How in hell can a man be a man and face such risks?

What is the punishment for mental cruelty? Divorce, loss of home and children, division of estate, alimony and lifelong servitude to the little woman any time she wants to haul you back into court for more child support and additional alimony.

With such a frightening prospect facing him, a man has one of two alternatives — never get married or submit, everytime, to the little lady's whims and desires. Never, but never, oppose her.

Of course, this condition can never produce a happy home. What woman wants a "Yes Ma'am" for a husband? So, eventually, divorce rolls around anyway. The tragedy lies in the fact that women are unhappy with their power and miserable with a weakling for a husband. Society, therefore, forces upon the female conditions which generate her own unhappiness. This crazy gift to women is actually a curse on both sexes.

Is it possible that men are no longer to be trusted? That in order to protect womanhood from abuses at the hands of the male population, society has given these rights to women to restore the balance?

The old concept that women are burdened by children and household chores and therefore immobile and helpless, is a thing of the past. As is the idea that all men are fickle and footloose.

Actually, the reversal of these concepts are nearer the truth. Through education, labor-saving devices, household help, money and cars, women are free of the ties which formerly held them captive to the homes. Conversely, in order to pay for all this, most men are hopelessly bound to their jobs — "Married to their jobs" as their wives complain.

Women today are highly mobile; men are almost completely immobilized. The wife may come and go as she chooses; the man is tied to his store or office. Powerful laws protect the helplessness of the immobilized sex. Which sex would qualify for this title today?

To label an entire sex untrustworthy is to abandon reason. The very training of the male invariably makes him a more responsible person than the female.

When people suddenly become rich through unexpected inheritance, or an actor is propelled overnight into instant stardom, a form of madness takes over and reason departs. Growth and character development fail to keep pace with sudden fame and fortune. Something breaks down and the recipient of largess begins to imagine that he has really earned it, and as a result, frequently loses it.

In a sense the female seeking divorce and distribution of the family community assets can be likened to such a type. Having played no part in the work invested in its making, she has no concept of its value in terms of its protection. She is, consequently, a victim of the madness which strikes anyone who finds himself suddenly in possession of large, unearned sums of money.

The husband, on the other hand, who labored diligently to amass the estate, knows its true worth. He has learned to adhere to business rules, written and unwritten. This experience and development hardly labels him as a person who is going to "rip off" his wife in a divorce settlement. And to suggest he will, as the law implies, is a debasement of his honor.

Granted, there are some husbands who are indifferent, who do abandon their families. But must we have vicious, crippling laws, universally enacted, to protect a few deserving individuals?

If community property and alimony laws are designed to protect the rights of women, in practice they achieve a totally opposite effect. Women's rights are best served by marriage, children and a husband whose honor and privilege it is to care for them. The stripping away of a man's position as head of the household and protector of his family and the vesting of this right in women eventually destroys the fulfillment women seek and need. Since, as a consequence their men become witless nonentities.

Abuses of the community property laws are transparent and subtle. Misuse is obvious in the case of the scheming female who sees in marriage a quick, easy road to riches. Tie the knot, spend a few years with the money-machine, provoke him into a verbal outburst (preferably in front of friends), head for the attorney, and unearned wealth — she can't lose. The law says so. But there are other evils and temptations more dangerous. When the law is equal and fair, judgment and appraisal of adversary rights are mandatory and many a rash act dies in its contemplative state. But, when the law is completely one-sided, why bother to weigh the consequences?

The law provides the women with a built-in no-lose situation. Have you ever heard of a man suing a woman for divorce on the grounds of mental cruelty? It rarely happens and when it does, the man is a laughing stock — it is not manly. This is solely a woman's perogative — she only is the victim of mental cruelty, never the author. And if a man did sue for divorce on such grounds, what would it gain him? He would still lose his home and children and have to pay alimony, child support and divide the community assets to boot. Is there any set of conditions whereby the male has the right to similarly punish the female in a divorce action and achieve some balance, some deterrent to make both parties pause before taking this step? The answer is no. Thousands of marriages might be saved were it not for this law which converts the male into a frightened apology of a man. Marriage is undoubtedly the most difficult of all human enterprises, but it could be the most rewarding. Two people living together have thousands of adjustments to make. The success of marriage, as in all enterprises comes with facing up to difficulties and working them out. There is no growth as individuals unless the inevitable problems are met and solved.

We have become sloppy in America. We want it all made easy and comfortable and the law obliges and makes it simple and attractive for the woman to end it all whenever she chooses and reap the profits of divorce.

What will it profit her if she gains the whole house, money and half the estate if it costs her her self respect and husband? But these consequences are hard to see. At this juncture the husband is an unfeeling bore. Even her friends tell her she is foolish to tolerate such a situation.

The choice becomes easy. Why not? Before marriage she had to work as secretary, saleslady or model. Now she can be financially secure, come and go as she pleases. She has respectability, her own home, her children. She answers to no one. Many a young lady rising at 7 a.m. on a Monday morning to go to work and returning at 6 p.m. to an empty apartment would love to trade places.

There are other areas where the male ego is eroded by such laws. California is the scene of much buying and selling of real estate. With many business and professional men, real estate becomes a secondary form of business.

But, in this enterprise a man requires his wife's signature on a real estate venture. The law says so. In his own business her permission is not required, but if he wants to buy a building to house his store, office or plant, he must obtain her consent. "What do you think, darling?" he asks. A foolish erosion of a man's self-esteem and respect for his own judgment.

Community property laws create a condition legally whereby the wife adds her opinion, an opinion not necessarily based upon knowledge, but frequently upon fear and inexperience. And she may withhold her consent for the same reasons.

The abuses of misplaced power vested in women create further hazards for the businessman involved in a divorce suit. During the early proceedings, a wife, exercising her rights on the advice of her attorney, can force her husband to agree to unreasonable temporary support, payments, by the simple expedient of tying up his bank account, business and real estate, sometimes to the eventual detriment of both parties.

For thousands of years men have been trusted to play their natural roles and the system has worked well. As a result men became more masculine and women more feminine. Now all this is reversed and the male, the former protector of his family, is replaced by the authority of the state who now becomes the protector of the wife.

Is this a boon for womanhood? The tragic results would hardly prove it so. This misplaced function of the state has resulted in the rapid demolition of the institution of marriage, has created as army of children minus fathers, an erosion of self-respect in the male and a growing but unwanted independence in the female.

The truth is that men are treated like errant schoolboys and wives are cast in the mold of mothers. To our Latin and European cousins this makes us ludicrous. The American female casts interested glances at the boldness of the Latin and the assertiveness of the European male, and the American male yearns for the submissiveness of the Latin and European female. American men and women look elsewhere for qualities they deny to each other.

The law conspires to make giants out of women and pygmies out of men. And laws, like most of the consumer goods in this country, are made by men for the selection and purchase of women. How far we have drifted from the practice of centuries when the estate remained in the family and was handed down from father to son always with the aim of growth and permanency.

There is no doubt that where the wife maintains the home front she has contributed equally toward the family fortune. Her courage and support certainly qualifies her for a share in the estate accumulated by the husband, in the event of divorce.

But too many women who claim their share at the time of a divorce have not performed the most elementary tasks associated with marriage, let alone accepted responsibilities above the call of duty. The husband drives himself to become a success using time that could more profitably be devoted to rest and recreation. He wants extra money to give his family a better way of life and more security. With some outstanding exceptions, wives of such men do a minimum of work in the home, are bored, petulant and resentful. Yet in divorce, they are legally entitled to alimony and one-half the community assets.

Some wives absent themselves from the home daily, leaving the children and husband to the tender mercies of the hired help. When challenged by the husband, who never married the maid in the first place, they say they have to do these things to be fulfilled. This fulfillment response evokes little protest from the husband — this is the unanswerable reply. Yet the obvious truth is that the wife has no intention of finding fulfillment in her marriage. Why the husband does not end the marriage then and there, I'll never know. He is supporting a parasite.

This desire of the female for fulfillment takes many forms. Some get jobs as models working for pin-money and admiration, some become actresses and others go all-out into vocations. Anything rather than be mother, wife and homemaker. Such women not only expect to be supported by their husbands in marriage, but demand rewards after marriage, in spite of their infidelity to the contract.

Picture a reverse situation. A hard working and devoted mother and wife. A husband bored by a monotonous job. He loves sailing. He only feels "fulfilled" when he is out sailing. A friend asks him if he would like to crew on a sailing trip to New Zealand. Be gone four months. No pay, just pleasure and fulfillment. He jumps at the chance. Will such a man be rewarded and applauded by society? His condemnation will be total — deserting his wife and kids.

Not all wives are delinquent. There are many who do their jobs as homemakers far beyond the limits expected of them — and find fulfillment too. Such wives rarely seek divorce. With half the income of other families their children are taken care of better, brought up-better; their homes sparkle with comfort and love, and the husband comes home at night to a restful, pleasurable experience.

Being a mother and a wife is a full-time job and requires aptitude and skills far beyond the needs of any career or profession. If she is truly a partner in the marriage, the wife gives as much on the home front as the husband does in business.

The wife who works to supplement her husband's income, often adequate, is something else. She comes home spent, sometimes later than her husband, weary and looking for comfort. Instead of massaging her husband's tired psyche, she wants to be comforted. The house is cheerless. The only female presence is that of the resentful maid.

It is popularly accepted that when the wife works it is unfair of the husband to expect to be taken care of in the so-called normal manner. Rather he should chip in and help with the marketing, cooking and housework. He is not only expected to forgo the comfort and relaxation he looks forward to when he comes home from work, but is expected to work around the house because his wife has an outside job. This may be fair in those cases where the wife must work — but in most instances, she doesn't have to. The doubtful advantage of her earnings, after taxes, translated into a new car or larger house, is no advantage at all compared to the real loss sustained by the husband and children through the absence of wife and mother. The economics of the family budget is watered down through energies directed elsewhere. Effort is reduced to a minimum and expediency at home is cultivated into a fine art.

In such circumstances, what does a man need a wife for?

There is no excuse. If a man earns $200 per week his wife and children will find more pleasure, comfort and happiness together than if she left the home to earn an additional $150 per week. (Lord help him if she ever earns more money than he!)

More examples of inequity: If a wife works during marriage, spends all her earnings on herself and devotes only part of her time — a fraction of what she should spend at home — she is still entitled to alimony and community property. She's entitled even if she spends no time at home. If, during the separation before divorce, she works, the husband must still contribute to her support. And if, during that time, he manages to save some of his earnings, the wife is entitled to half these savings too.

Example: Husband and wife both work during separation period. He earns $1,500 a month, she $1,000. His temporary support payments are $500, leaving him $1,000. If he lives on $500 and saves $500, he must pay his wife half the savings, or $250. She then totals $1,000 plus $500, plus $250, or $1,750. The husband has $750.

The law says the wife may keep all the money she earns during the pre-trial period. It is not community property. The husband's savings are community property. A strange situation. Thrift is part of the American success story but, under such circumstances, a man is better off to work as little as possible and spend everything he makes.

In fact, under our present system, the spectacle of a successful businessman driving himself to ulcers and an early grave is sheer lunacy. His achievements usually spell total failure in the living department. Because of the wisdom of the law, the only practical method a man can adopt to decrease the possibility of being stripped by his wife in divorce is to stop working when he has enough. Stop the acceleration. Save nothing. Spend it all. Enjoy it here and now.

There are rewards enough awaiting such a brave man. With no estate to divide, his wife will reflect carefully before leaping into divorce. Her attorney will view the meager pickings with a jaundiced eye, and unctuously advise the little woman to stay with her husband and work things out. But this isn't all. As the husband develops his ability to earn the same amount of money in less time, he will be able to cut his work week to four, to three, to even one day a week. *No judge can reprimand him for that!*

What will he do with the rest of his time? Why, he will enjoy life. Fish, hunt, paint and develop a multitude of exciting avocations, golf, tennis, camping — all aimed at the prolongation of his life, the improvement of his health and an increase in his well-being.

He needn't labor half a lifetime in some office, factory or store, missing the good things in life, only to awaken one morning to find his wife, home and children gone, half his money gone and all his efforts wasted.

Not only will the slim pickings act as a deterrent to his wife and her attorney, but the chances are that he will be a better husband and father — the sort of man a woman would never want to leave.

So many rich men's wives complain that their husbands are married to their work — they never do anything together. With this new concept of living, husband and wife would spend more time together and develop mutual interests. Husband would no longer be the overworked money-machine, but a relaxed, interesting companion.

Laws are made in equity to benefit the majority. To maintain such rules, punishments are devised to discipline the intransigent. Criminals are jailed and violators are fined and/or imprisoned. That, of course, is the theory and, for the most part, it works well, with one glaring exception.

These noble concepts fall to pieces in the one area where justice is most desperately needed — at the dissolution of a marriage and in the application of alimony, community property, and child custody laws. Hence, the chaos in marriage and divorce.

An embezzler goes to jail when he is apprehended — he is not honored. A malpractitioner loses his license — he is not given a testimonial dinner. The deserter is court-martialed and disgraced — he is not promoted. It is assumed that the perpetrators of these misdeeds knew what they were doing, had a fair hearing and were aware of the consequences.

But, when it comes to marriage, society throws away all its experience and good sense. Society, supported by a passive male population, has a simple rule: In divorce someone must suffer and it is better that the someone not be a woman.

Were one to suggest that no divorce be granted unless it was equitably contested and that out-of-court settlements be disallowed, the outcry would be tremendous. Platitudes would rain down, fast and thick.

"You can't keep people together if they want to separate." "You can't make a woman live with a man if she doesn't want to." "Better an out-of-court settlement than a bloody court fight." And so on ad nauseam.

I am afraid we have been too hasty in providing an easy solution to this difficult problem. We have chosen what appears to be the quick way out as an answer to our social malaise. As a result, we have no solution at all and a growing social sickness that threatens to pull down the entire fabric of marriage and home.

If home, family and two parents for children are important — and they must be if the nation is to endure — then divorce must be treated as a national emergency. If society is at fault in allowing marriage to take place frivolosuly, without training or planning, then it must not allow divorce to take place equally frivolously.

Anyone who has sat through an hour of non-contested divorce hearings in a court room knows how farcical is the procedure. There are five players, the wife, the judge, the wife's witness and two attorneys. After a number of cases, each taking about ten minutes, one gets the impression that one is listening to a dull, hometown, amateur, theatrical company rehearsing the same scene over and over again. The law loses its majesty, the courtroom disappears and becomes a backdrop for a put-up job. The judge is stripped of his dignity and must, with resignation, listen to a well-rehearsed scene where the conclusions are foregone. He then renders his decision, a decision he knows he is going to make before the courtroom travesty began.

When justice is reduced to a mechanical rote, the results must be far-reaching and dangerous. All divorce cases should be tried. Any attempt to evade this by collusion and pre-trial agreement should be treated as contempt of court.

If society really wants to cut the appalling divorce rate and reduce the vast number of children from broken homes, it must insist on proper preparation for marriage and make the decision a very serious one. And it must judge the divorce action in exactly the same way as any other court action.

If evidence indicates that the wife is responsible for the marriage break-up, has been delinquent in her responsibilities and duties, then she should be denied the divorce unless she chooses to lose home and children to the husband and forfeit alimony and community property. Alternatively, if the evidence proves the husband to be the prime mover in the disintegration of the marriage, then the wife should be granted the divorce along with the home, children, support, alimony and share of the community property. Between these extremes there may be a thousand modifications.

I wager there would be fewer divorces and a marked improvement in the preparation for marriage. There would also be a greater willingness on the part of the husband and wife to overcome their problems and make the marriage work.

Attorney's fees should be limited by law and not provide them with a powerful incentive to heap coals on burning fires for their own interest and profit.

If this perversion of justice, as it occurs in marriage and divorce, applied in business and commerce, the nation's economy would come to a grinding halt. Picture a businessman being sued for half his business and salary for life by an ex-employee who, having showed up late for work and who, having pulled only half his weight, resigned because he didn't care to have the boss question him about his laziness. Picture the same businessman taking on a partner minus capital. The partner is supposed to perform certain functions and fails to do so. The businessman complains whereupon the partner in a huff, hies himself to an attorney, sues and collects half the business' profits for life and his attorney's fees to boot.

A man honors a woman when he marries her. That, at least, was the traditional concept. Why, then, is he treated worse than a criminal when his wife divorces him? A criminal receives equity in law — a fair trial with acquittal or conviction and sentence subject to parole.

Husbands, during divorce, are treated like criminals by the wife's attorney, receive no trial, have no chance of acquittal and no hope of parole. Is it because the husband has the misfortune to be the breadwinner? If that is true we had better look again, because women are gaining in this direction.

A woman seeks a divorce. Fine, if she wants it, let her have it — and pay for it too. Since she gets the divorce she demands custody of the children. Why? Well, she is the mother you know. She may be working more hours at a job outside the home than the husband, but she still gets the kids. And since she gets the children, she must have the house. Since she gets the house, she has to receive alimony to support it and child support for the children.

Now the husband has lost everything, and has the privilege of paying for everything he has lost. If a man remarried every time he was sued for divorce, I wonder how many homes he could afford to lose, how much alimony, child support and community property he could give away before he decided to leave the country and join the Foreign Legion?

Fancy being evicted from your home, by the mortgage holder who didn't like the way you said good morning and then being forced to pay the mortgage the rest of your life and maintain the house to boot.

However, the end is not yet in sight. If we haven't yet made a travesty of marriage, let us take one more step and complete the farce.

After spending months, sometimes years and a fortune in attorney's fees, not to mention the wear and tear on the human frame to create a divorce settlement, we now find that this most difficult of all contracts is not a contract at all. Any time the ex-wife chooses, she can haul her ex-mate into court and ask for a change in the agreement. All she has to do is hire an attorney (the ex-husband pays) and request that alimony and child support be increased. Of course she may on occasion lose, nevertheless the prospect of being brought again to court, hiring an attorney, preparing a defense with all its emotional drain, faces all husbands who sire children.

This threat can hound the ex-husband for the rest of his life and destroy whatever hope he may have for future happiness. The case is never ended. The debt is never fully paid. No criminal is ever treated like this unless he compounds his felony by getting married.

In all areas of life where a contract is drawn between people, the pact implies a future obligation. The contract usually follows negotiation and compromise on the part of the signatories. It guarantees performance for the future, never the present or past. A signatory to a contract recognizes that some unilateral need may occur in the future, but is willing to forego these wants for the sake of the mutual benefits bestowed by the contract.

Woe betide the party who breaks the contract. His tenure as a businessman will be short-lived. Laws are devised to protect contracts and the law stands ready to rule on damages incurred by the injured party.

But, unfortunately, in the all-important areas of contracts regarding alimony and child support, the female like Caesar's wife, is above the law and can, at any time, request a change in the contract which has been achieved at great cost. What good, therefore, is such a contract? What use for a husband to spend months negotiating a settlement that won't last?

We should take a lesson from the Greeks. Aristophanes' *Lysistrata* organized the women of Athens to institute a sex strike to deter their men who were forever fighting in the wars with Sparta. The Athenian women barricaded themselves inside the Capital and refused to come out until their husbands promised to give up fighting and stay home. It worked! When they saw their wives were adamant, the men eventually decided they would rather fuck than fight. So they gave up warring and returned to the loving arms of their wives.

Men should do a *Lysistrata* in marriage — universally refrain from marriage until women desire and learn to be wives, mothers and homemakers. And lawmakers devise new laws that make man once more the head of the household with the rights he enjoyed and exercised until sixty years ago.

No change in law — no marriage!

Simple as that!

Our lawmakers would be well advised to hearken to that great English sage Dr. Samuel Johnson who said over two hundred and fifty years ago: *"Sir, nature has given women so much power that the law cannot afford to give her more."*

Life continues, people fall in love, marry, have children and get divorced and still this specter haunts our land in every state, city and home. How blithely we accept it. We fight sickness in hospitals and research laboratories; churches pontificate on ways of improving the spiritual needs of the people, and councils discuss highways and sanitation. Governments declare war on poverty and, periodically, try to right civil wrongs — but no one declares war on divorce, broken homes and the plight of fatherless children. A few brave attorneys, judges and sociologists have attempted to revise our divorce laws, but they were doomed to failure by gutless legislatures more interested in votes than human welfare.

We build better schools, press for higher wages, and put our creative and technological skills into the production of more comfort and leisure. We gild the lily in a thousand ways and neglect the fact that the flower is slowly dying.

What makes us so aware of the need for a new car, new clothes, new homes and yet sees us so complacent and unaware of the crying need to reform our divorce laws so that men and women may live with their children in holy matrimony as a family? Not for two or three or five years but through all the blessed experience of life as lovers, parents and grandparents.

We are one nation yet we have different laws for different states. We condone cheating, collusion in divorce and ignore the transparent "Quickies" of Florida and Nevada.

Without the family and the home there is no nation. If, 150 years ago, our divorce rate had equaled that of today, there would be no America. How long will you wait, America, before you apply your great inventive skills to the solution of this, America's most terrifying problem?

The California State Legislature, alarmed by the appalling increase in divorce, and finally acknowledging that marriage and divorce laws had not changed since 1872, grappled for years to amend these laws to avert a growing national disaster. Two bills were enacted by the legislature in 1969. They were as effective as a chain-link fence in containing an advancing glacier.

1967, pre new FAMILY LAW ACT of 1969:
..divorce rate   42.66%
1970, first year of new law ..divorce rate   80.62%
1975, sixth year of new law ..divorce rate 105.81%

APPENDIX

At the start of this book I suggested that introductions should be placed and read at the end of a book. Today I have a growing conviction that research should be done **after** the book has been written. If this sounds like putting the cart before the horse let us examine some current trends in writing and research.

We have become slaves to research. We religiously examine all aspects of human behavior. In this rush to probe all facts, figures and minutiae we are, I believe, losing sight of basic human intelligence, intuition, observation, selectivity and confidence in our own judgment; we defer all to the so-called "experts."

The writer's growing dependency on research frequently obscures his original concept. His inspiration can become buried under a welter of facts, notes and the "expert findings" of others.

Recently I read a book which purported to investigate the hidden psychological barriers to successful collective bargaining. Written by two young professionals, it was a masterpiece of research and, academically no doubt, a scholastic achievement. Each of the 350 pages contained from three to six references. It was impossible to follow the thread of the authors' thesis. Each reference dutifully cited author, title, publisher, city and year.

The bibliography ran to 35 pages, listing an impressive total of 1400 books — surely a research record and a lifetime challenge to the serious student of industrial bargaining. At the rate of three books a week it would take nine years for the reader to authenticate the authors' findings.

I did not read the 1400 books but I did note the earth-shattering findings uncovered by the two psychologist-authors after their herculean labors.

There were two massive break-throughs:

When parties arrive at the negotiating table with more than one problem to be discussed, negotiations may take longer!

And:

When parties to an industrial dispute meet to negotiate, forearmed with distrust and anger, compromise and settlement may be more difficult to achieve!

These revelations were not completely accepted by the authors despite their massive research for they went on to say:

These conclusions have not been arrived at by our own research but are the findings of Professor --------- and will require our own independent investigation to prove these points.

The research for "Marriage — Grounds for Divorce" was done **after** the book was written, in fact 11 years later. The book was written between 1962 and 1965 and edited in 1976 and then, and only then, in the autumn of 1976, did I write to the California state government at Sacramento for data and statistics on marriage and divorce.

The following material was obtained from The Office of Research, California State Assembly.

TABLE A

POPULATION, MARRIAGES, DIVORCES AND ANNULMENTS, CALIFORNIA 1922 - 1975

Date	Population	Marriages	*Rate	Divorces	** %
1922	3,991,000	47,477	11.90	9,227	19.40
1927	5,147,000	53,487	10.40	14,135	26.40
1932	5,849,000	43,164	7.30	14,097	32.67
1937	6,528,000	69,397	9.90	20,718	29.14
1942	7,735,000	76,014	9.80	22,962	30.00
1947	9,832,000	94,461	9.60	45,997	48.70
1952	11,638,000	78,883	6.80	36,682	46.50
1962	16,638,000	114,128	6.80	48,027	42.00
1967	19,232,000	150,000	7.80	63,139	42.66
		— — —			
1970	19,680,000	172,388	8.75	***138,953	80.62
1971	20,292,900	168,049	8.22	143,464	85.36
1972	20,517,900	175,918	8.56	143,793	81.75
1973	20,741,000	169,319	8.13	152,367	90.00
1974	20,963,500	160,882	7.60	160,613	100.00
1975	21,205,900	154,803	7.32	163,801	105.81

NOTE: California New Family Law Act Commences January 1, 1970.

*   Rates are per 1000 population

**   Percentage of number of divorces to number of marriages in that year.

***   Initial complaint for divorce; should not be confused with final decrees of divorce.

DECLINE OF MARRIAGE

Since 1922 the rate of marriage per thousand in the population declines from 11.90 for that year to 7.32 in 1975 — 38.40%

Since 1922 the percentage of divorces to marriages has risen from 19.40% in that year to *105.81% for the year 1975 — 544%

*Initial Complaint for Divorce

In 1970 the first year of the New California Divorce Laws the number of initial complaints for divorce were more than double the initial complaints for 1967.

Between 1970 and 1975 there was a population increase in the state of 1,152,900, yet in 1975 there were 17,585 fewer marriages than in 1970.

```
1970 POPULATION 19,680,000  MARRIAGES ..... 172,388
1975 POPULATION 21,205,900  MARRIAGES ..... 154,803

1975 POPULATION INCREASE ................. 7.75%
1975 MARRIAGE DECLINE .................... 16.30%
```

According to Time Magazine (Dec. 1976) " . . . . . . there are more people in the 21 - 30 age group in the state (California) living together than are actually married."

Age group 21 - 30 is traditionally the largest section of the population where marriages take place.

. . . .

STATISTIC SOURCES: U.S. Bureau of Census. PC (1) -B6

U.S. Bureau of Census *Current Population Reports* Series P-25, No. 139.

State of California, Department of Finance, *California Population Characteristics, 1962* and *Population Estimates for California Counties, April 28, 1971 and August 18, 1972.*

Records of Ex-Officio clerks of the Superior Courts. State of California, Department of Health, Birth, Death, Marriage and Divorce Records.

"SUFFER LITTLE CHILDREN . . ."

CHILDREN FROM DIVORCING PARENTS . . . . 1970 to 1975
IN COMPARISON TO NUMBER OF MARRIAGES FOR THOSE
YEARS.

Year	Marriages	Divorces	Children	Involved
1970	172,388	138,953	188,704	*110.00%
1971	168,049	143,464	192,692	114.70%
1972	175,918	143,793	188,168	107.00%
1973	169,319	152,367	190,107	112.28%
1974	160,882	160,613	193,709	120.50%
1975	154,803	163,801	194,208	125.45%

*Percentage of children from divorcing parents to marriages.

Total marriages — 1970 through 1975 1,001,359
Children: divorcing parents, same period 1,147,588
114.00% more children than marriages in six years.

California child population, 1975 . . . . *6,833,490
Children — divorced parents 1966 - 1975 . . . . *1,794,442
Percentage of children — divorced parents, ten year total, to California child population — 1975 . . . . 26.25%

*Zero to eighteen years.

DIVORCE . . . . . DISSOLUTION OF MARRIAGE
MENTAL CRUELTY . . .
IRRECONCILABLE DIFFERENCES

Prior to the passage of the California New Family Law Act in 1969 the traditional grounds for divorce employed by wives was EXTREME CRUELTY (mental cruelty). In 1969, the last year this term was used, it accounted for 95.83 per cent of all grounds for divorce for that year.

The New Family Law Act changed all grounds for divorce to "Irreconcilable Differences" and incurable insanity. "Dissolution of Marriage" replaces the term Divorce.

1969 — Divorces 120,985	Mental Cruelty . 113,633 —— 95.83%		
1970 — Diss/Marriage 138,953	Irrec/Diff 132,823 —— 95.00%		
1971 — Diss/Marriage 143,664	Irrec/Diff 138,579 —— 96.00%		
1972 — Diss/Marriage 143,793	Irrec/Diff 139,287 —— 97.00%		
1973 — Diss/Marriage 152,367	Irrec/Diff 148,231 —— 97.24%		
1974 — Diss/Marriage 160,613	Irrec/Diff 156,885 —— 97.63%		
1975 — Diss/Marriage 163,801	Irrec/Diff 159,393 —— 97.31%		

These figures show a remarkable similarity regardless of the change in the nomenclature for divorce and mental cruelty. In fact if we transpose the terms, "Dissolution of Marriage" and "Irreconcilable Differences" for Divorce and Mental Cruelty we must admit nothing has changed.

POPULATION-MARRIAGES-DIVORCES U.S.A.
1972 - 1976

Year	Population	Marriages	Divorces	Percentages
1972	208,234,000	2,282,000	845,000	37.00%
1973	209,859,000	2,284,000	915,000	40.00%
1974	211,389,000	2,229,000	977,000	43.00%
1975	213,137,000	2,126,000	1,026,000	48.26%
1976	214,500,000	2,133,000	1,077,000	50.00%

Population increases: 1972-1976 6,266,000 3.00%
Number of marriages decline: 1972-1976   149,000 6.53%
Number of divorces increase: 1972-1976   232,000 27.36%

Child Population, U.S.A. 1975 70,522,000
Children — Divorced Parents,
   10 year period, 1965-1974 .... * 8,609,000 (12.24%)

Commencing in 1974, divorces for that year and each successive year reached more than twice the national total at the beginning of the decade; 1965 — 479,000.

*Zero to eighteen years of age.

SOURCE: Department of Health, Education and Welfare
National Center for Health Statistics
Health Resources Administration.
Division of Vital Statistics.

EXCERPTS FROM CALIFORNIA LEGISLATURE — 1969 REGULAR SESSION — ASSEMBLY COMMITTEE REPORT ON ASSEMBLY BILL NO. 530 AND SENATE BILL NO. 252 (THE FAMILY LAW ACT)

James A. Hayes, Chairman,
Assembly Committee on Judiciary

"California's outmoded divorce laws, *dating for the most part from 1872,* lately have generated considerable dissatisfaction. . . . Governor Edmund G. Brown, in May, 1966, established the Governor's Commission on the Family to examine what he termed *'The high incidence of divorce in our society and* its often tragic consequences.' The Commission was charged with four principal responsibilities: First, to study and suggest revision, when necessary of the substantive laws of California relating to the family; Second, to determine the feasibility of developing significant and meaningful courses in family life education to be offered in the public schools; Third, to consider the possibility and desirability of developing uniform nationwide standards of marriage and divorce jurisdiction; and Fourth, to examine the establishment of Family Courts on a statewide basis . . . . ''

(author's italics)

In December 1966 the commission published its final report. From that date until the adoption of the FAMILY LAW ACT of 1969 by the California State Assembly this report was subjected to a great deal of controversy, changes, amendments and general butchery. It finally emerged as —

A B 530 (Hayes — Chapter 1609, Statutes of 1969) and

S B 252 (Grunsky — Chapter 16008 — Statutes of 1969)

Many problems and controversies plagued the preparation of the original committee's report. New Bills were introduced during the 1967 sessions of the California Legislature (A B 1420 Shoemaker and S B 826 Grunsky) which embodied the recommendations of the Commission. These bills ran into further problems which made passage unlikely. An alternative bill, A B 487 (Hayes) was therefore introduced in 1968. This bill, like its predecessors, was held in committee FOR FURTHER STUDY.

Among the proposals of the Governor's Commission was the setting up of a —

" . . . state-wide family court with jurisdiction over all matters pertaining to the family, including marriage, divorce (dissolution of marriage), guardianship etc. The family court was to be equipped with a fully-trained professional staff. Under the commission plan, upon the filing of a petition to dissolve the marriage, the clerk would fix the date for interviews at which the parties and a member of the professional staff would explore the desirability of continuing the marriage. Attendance of the parties at one of the interviews was a condition precedent to any further proceedings, and failure to obey a court order to attend would result in contempt.

Upon receiving the report of the staff, the court could either order further counseling for a period not exceeding 60 days or set a hearing date and proceed with dissolution. At the hearing the court would be empowered to continue the proceedings for up to 90 days to allow the parties to avail themselves of additional counseling. If, at the end of that period reconciliation had not been effected, the court was mandated, under the commission's proposal, to enter a decree dissolving the marriage upon application of either party.

Dissolution was to be based upon the sole findings by the court that legitimate objects of matrimony have been destroyed and that there is no reasonable likelihood that the marriage can be saved."

BUT THIS WAS NOT TO BE . . . .

"The bill, introduced in 1969 which contained the family court proposal (S B 252), was modified to the extent that only an *initial interview* was mandatory. Proponents argued that such an "interview" with a highly trained counselor would be for the purposes of gathering rudimentary information only. Subsequent sessions with the trained counselor were to be *voluntary*.

In summary, as seen by the Governor's Commission, proceedings for the dissolution of marriage were to be for the purpose of inquiring into the marriage and determining whether it could be saved. *There was to be no adversary proceedings* in which any fault on the part of one of the parties would be germane. The report of the counselors would be determinative, rather than the testimony of the parties themselves. *Apparently, counseling was thought to be necessary because of its supposed therapeutic value in aiding family stability* . . .

For several reasons the proposal of the Governor's Commission with respect to mandatory counseling was unacceptable to the Assembly Judiciary Committee during the three years it was considered. Some of these reasons were: (1) Counseling by its very nature is not likely to be effective in a marital situation unless both spouses are willing; (2) when counseling is voluntarily undertaken it is more likely to produce reconciliation because the parties, by agreeing to sit and discuss problems, indicate some willingness to save the marriage."
(author's italics)

The Assembly Judiciary Committee failed to understand that parties to a divorce action have, by this time, reached such a state of emotional stress and recrimination that the chances of goodwill and reason prevailing at this juncture to induce them to accept counseling on a voluntary, mutually agreeable basis, are indeed very slight.

It was argued that the state should be SLOW to inject itself into matters of private concern.

" . . . marriage," it continued, "is a private and personal relationship in which the state should not interfere by forcing the spouses to disclose their most confidential secrets to a third party as the price of dissolution."

BUT THE BIG REASON WAS:

Mandatory counseling was rejected because of its potential cost to the state.

" . . . It was estimated that it would cost the counties $10,000,000 per year. That is a heavy price to pay when no evidence established that counseling would have any significant effect upon family stability. Furthermore, it was evident that sufficient counseling personnel with the qualifications and experience required by the bill, could not be found to staff the family court in the foreseeable future."

Evidently, the opponents of the bill had not closely followed previous commentaries on the divorce situation in California. At a hearing, held in Los Angeles in January 8-9, 1964, to inquire into divorce reform, Judge Rodger Pfaff, presiding judge of the Consolidated Conciliation and Domestic Relation Court of Los Angeles County, testified as follows:

" . . . . . about 98 or 99 per cent of divorces today are by default. There is no advance procedure in the overwhelming majority of these cases. Moreover, 90 percent of these are neither necessary nor justified, that is, provided these people could actually have some counseling and were interested in saving their marriage. We have found that where we can persuade them to take advantage of the reconciliation court's facilities . . . that 64 out of 100 couples reconciled. A year later, 3 out of every 4 of them were still together."

However, we can add that the social, sexual and societal influences that doom marriage from the outset would not be influenced by all these investigations, committees and proposed laws. Therefore, the steamroller of divorce would proceed on its way gathering an ever increasing momentum. Figures on divorce applications '70 to '75 shows this to be true.

THE FOLLOWING ARE THE NEW LAWS OF CALIFORNIA
GOVERNING MARRIAGE AND DIVORCE, PASSED IN
1969 TOGETHER WITH NINE LAWS PASSED IN 1975-76

The new laws affecting marriage and divorce are the results of investigations, committees, factfinding and, above all, much research dating back to 1963. In that year, Assemblyman Pearce Young, author of three unsuccessful bills relating to domestic relations, started a movement to initiate a study to " . . . identify problem areas and gather information with a view towards developing a legislative program to strengthen family relations." As a result, House Resolution 234 was passed on April 18th, 1963. The intent of this Resolution was to create an appropriate interim committee to study the feasibility of enacting standards for the guidance of the judiciary in the application of existing civil code procedures relating to divorce, alimony, support, and custody of children. From this early beginning to the final passage of the Family Law Act of 1969, six years later, eminent men wrestled with the overwhelming and growing problem of divorce and struggled to find a solution. After many meetings, discussions, changes, resolutions and amendments the California state legislature, together with experts of every kind, including members of the judiciary, and the California Bar Association came up with an aspirin to cure a social cancer. Its effectiveness may be judged by figures which appear in this appendix which reveal that *divorce, instead of decreasing through the beneficence of these new laws actually *rose from 138,953 in 1970 – or 80 percent of the marriages for that year, to 163,801 – or 106 per cent of marriages in 1975.* There were 154,803 marriages in 1975. This figure is again significant for, in comparison with the figures for 1970, it represents a drop in marriages of 17,505 or 11.3 per cent. This decline in marriages took place in spite of an increase in the population of California from 1970 to 1975 of over one and a half million people.

*Initial complaint for divorce, annulment and separate maintenance.

Main features of California's New Divorce Laws
  A B 530 (Hayes — chapter 1609 *Statutes of 1969*)
  S B 252 (Grunsky — chapter 1608, *Statutes of 1969*)

Under the former divorce laws *matrimonial offense* or *fault* formed the basis of California divorce law. Causes included adultery, extreme cruelty, willful desertion, habitual intemperance, willful neglect or conviction of a felony. Plaintiff had to prove that his or her spouse had committed a specific offense. Under the old law, about 95 per cent of complaints were based upon the most general ground of fault, **extreme cruelty. The Family Law Act creates two grounds for marital dissolution:

"irreconcilable differences which have caused the irremediable breakdown in marriage, and incurable insanity".

The name of the action is changed from *divorce* to *dissolution of marriage*. Parties are called *petitioner and respondent* rather than *plaintiff and defendant*.

New law reduces waiting period for final decree from 12 months to 6 months.

Property Division: the concept of "fault" is eliminated as a basis for determining the amounts of community property each spouse is awarded. Instead the Act provides "the court shall . . . divide the community property equally" *regardless of bad conduct or economic need of the parties.*

Spousal Support: the Act provides: the Court may order a party to pay for the support of the other party **any amount** and for such period of time, as the court may deem just and reasonable having regard for the circumstances of the respective parties, including the duration of the marriage, and the ability of the supported spouse to engage in gainful employment.

**mental cruelty

Child Custody: under the Act, as under the old law, child custody is still to be determined **"according to the best interests of the child. In order to discourage husbands from contesting custody, the new law retains the maternal preference for young children."**

Based upon the foregoing, it must be admitted that little has changed. After so many years in the making, the new divorce laws fall far short of offering a minimum solution to California's divorce problems. One of the most important suggestions, compulsory attendance of the family court and counseling was eliminated as too costly a procedure and an interference in the private affairs of the parties. The name of the action has been changed but the disease continues to flourish. Division of community property still vests a power in the female that must render even the strongest male impotent. Note above: *"the court may divide the property equally regardless of bad conduct . . . "* This, of course, will give a moral boost to unscrupulous wives delinquent in their marital responsibilities. The evil aspects of the automatic giving of child custody remains the same. While repeating parrot fashion that old saw, *the best interests of the child,* the law admits it actually intends to discourage husbands from contesting custody.

Bills Enacted 1975-76 Session of
California Legislature

A B 460 (Maddy Chapter 35 — Marriage)

Eliminates evidence of specific misconduct in Court for dissolution of marriage or legal separation including depositions and discovery proceedings, except where child custody is issue and such evidence is relevant to that issue.

A B 1747 (Maddy Chapter 130 re: — Civil Law)

Old law required husband not to be responsible to maintain wife's children by former marriage. New law would extend this provision to either spouse. Old law provides that every man shall support his wife and his child, and his parent when in need; every woman is required to support her child, and her husband and her parent, when in need. This bill instead provides that every person shall support his/her spouse, child or parent when in need.

A B 3328 Relates to a reduction in the size of population of a county in order to qualify the county clerk as a commissioner of marriage.

A B 3627 Relates to fees for filing dissolution of marriage, issuing marriage, etc.

A B 555 Provides for wives to request, at divorce, former or birth name, as compared to old law which automatically gave wives former name at time of divorce. It prohibits any business or service from refusing to do business with female who uses maiden name, in divorce — and regardless of her marital status.

S B 736 Pertains to attorney's fees and costs awarded to petitioner to have marriage adjudged void — where such a party is innocent of fraud of wrong-doing in entering the marriage.

S B 1194 Under existing law, upon the application of a party to a proceeding related to determination of a void or voidable marriage or dissolution of marriage, the superior court is authorized to issue an ex parte order enjoining any party from molesting or disturbing the peace of the other party. This bill would extend the authorized scope of such an order to include enjoinment of the molestation or disturbance *of any person under the care, custody or control of the other party.*

". . . During the pendency of any proceeding under title 2 or title 3 of this part, upon application of *either* party in the manner provided by Section 527 of the Code of Civil Procedure, the superior court may issue ex parte orders (1) restraining *any party* person from transferring, encumbering, hypothecating, concealing, or in any way disposing of any property, real or personal, whether community or quasi-community, *or separate,* except in the usual course of business or for the necessities of life, and if such order is directed against a party, requiring him to notify the other party of such proposed expenditures and to account to the court for all such extraordinary expenditures; (2) enjoining any party from *molesting or disturbing the peace of the other party or any person under the control of the party:* (3) excluding *either party* from the *family dwelling or from the dwelling of other* upon a showing that physical or *emotional harm* would otherwise result, as provided in section 5102; and (4) *determining the temporary custody* of any minor children of the marriage.''

S˙ B 2005 This Bill would require the court to value assets and liabilities as near as practicable to the time of trial, except that upon specified 30 days notice, the court, for good cause shown, is authorized to value all or any portion of the assets and liabilities at a date after separation and prior to trial to accomplish an equal division in an equitable manner. In addition: Where economic circumstances warrant, the court may award *any asset* to one party on such conditions as it deems proper to effect a substantially equal division of the property. As an additional award or offset against existing property, the court may award, from a party's share, *any sums* it determines to have been deliberately misappropriated by such party to the exclusion of the community property or quasi-community property interest of the other party.

S B 2038 This Bill would require the State Department of Health to prepare and publish a brochure regarding genetic defects and diseases. The department would be required to distribute a copy of it to all applicants for a marriage license.
(author's italics)

Comments on S B 1194 and S B 2005

Of the nine Bills affecting marriage, passed by the 1975-76 Session of the California Legislature, S B 1194 and S B 2005 are the only ones that make any significant contribution to the present desperate state of California marriage and divorce — and such contributions are — all bad.

While I will acknowledge that the originators of these Bills and their enactors in the Legislature had the best intentions, I fail to see how incorporation into law of these two Bills will not inflame and aggravate an already incendiary situation. Good intentions are not enough. When the passions are aroused, as they are in divorce, deep insights into the workings of human behavior are of the highest importance.

One of the biggest problems with the pre-1970 marriage and divorce laws was not just the law but the abuse to which it was subjected by many wives and their lawyers who bent the law to their own ends. Of course this abuse is not endemic to marital laws but extends to most laws which are remolded (within the law) to suit the needs of powerful people, companies and their lawyers. One would be hard pressed to say who is more culpable in these cases, the client or the lawyer.

In divorce, where community property of appreciable amounts, child custody and visitation rights are involved, these two laws hand the traditional abusers of the marital and divorce laws — the wife and her attorney — an even larger club with which to press for unfair advantage.

Part (1) of S B 1194, " . . . *restraining any person from transferring etc.*" Without any doubt the **any person** is going to be the husband. And the party making the application for restraint is going to be the wife. The law may cast a thin film of neutrality over the wording by the employment of the phrase, **any person** or **either party,** but it is going to be the wife in concert with her lawyer who is going to be the **moving party.** Whenever the soon-to-be-shed husband does not accede to unreasonable demands foisted upon him by his wife's attorney his entire business can be tied up and the jugular vein squeezed tight. Of course his business is supposedly excluded from this provision, but, in many cases, the line between a business asset and a personal one is thin. Of course, the husband can go to court and prove the particular asset that the wife has asked to be frozen *is in the usual course of business.* And he might win. But meanwhile he has had more aggravation, more loss of time, more expenses and more reason to hate his wife. Note this section of the law also includes *separate property* — that is, property acquired before the marriage took place. We can expect a real brouhaha over this one. Certainly these new conditions do not reduce the normal tensions occuring in divorce; they will exacerbate them.

Part (2) "enjoining **any party** from molesting . . . any person under the care, custody . . . etc." Should the wife decide not to give the children to the father on his visiting day, he must retire from the scene like a good little boy. We can expect many a wife to take full advantage of this provision should she be irked at her ex-husband *for some other cause.* We can also expect fathers to grow more manly as a consequence — and lawyers, busier.

Part (3) Excluding "either party from the family dwelling . . . upon showing that physical or emotional harm would otherwise result etc." Well, we know who will want to have the family dwelling and we know, further, which sex is more likely to experience *emotional harm.* Under the old law 95 per cent of all complaints for divorce were based upon "extreme cruelty" (mental cruelty) and the vast majority of these sufferers were wives. In *Wendall H. Goddard's prize winning essay, **"A Report On California's New Divorce Laws: Progress and Problems," he says, "In uncontested cases, the plaintiff proved the defendant's guilt (mental cruelty) by simply testifying that the defendant's *cold and indifferent* behavior has caused the plaintiff to become *seriously ill, nervous and upset.* A witness corroborated this testimony, and the legal charade was complete. In contested cases the courts required more conclusive evidence of misconduct. Fault finding proceedings often consumed many days and usually aggravated an already deteriorated relationship between the parties. Only after *one spouse* was found guilty would the court grant a divorce.

"Such fault-based divorce received increasingly severe criticism. The main objection was that the fault concept was unrelated to the real cause of marital failure. Only rarely would a single act of fault cause total breakdown of the marriage: in most cases both spouses were responsible for the act of misconduct . . . A second objection to the fault theory was that it encouraged bitterness and animosity between the parties. The law's insistence on proving guilt coupled with the use of *adversary techniques* in family litigation intensified conflict between the parties and resulted in psychological damage to the children."

Since lawyers will plead for the petitioners in matters affected by this new law and judges will try the hearings and, since we know that lawyers and judges have not changed that much since the days of *mental cruelty,* we can expect the earlier abuses to continue.

S B 2005 . . . requires the court to value assets and liabilities as near as practicable to the time of trial . . . or on 30 days notice by the *moving party* to the *other party,* etc. Based upon all previous experience of the heavy role played by the little

*Third year student, University of California School of Law, Berkeley, California.

**This article won second prize in the Howard C. Schwab Memorial Essay contest.

woman and her legal counsel in divorce, we can expect the fashioning of still more clubs with which to beat the husband into submission. Many businesses experience a fluctuating rise and fall of assets; vengeful wives can seize upon a temporary rise in a husband's business assets (stocks), get the value of the community assets fixed and collect an unreasonable sum even if the assets should fall, at the time of divorce, far short of the previously established figure.

As an additional award or offset against existing property, the court may award, from a party's share, *any sum it determines to have been deliberately misappropriated etc.* Notice it reads "any sum." We can expect some real harmony when the divorcing wife, always a model of reason and fair play, has some friend whisper in her ear that her husband has been deceiving her and secretly stashing away large sums of money. We can also expect attorney's fees to swell as each side tries to prove the **TRUTH.**

In conclusion, it must be apparent to all that if so much of the marital strife that exists in California and the emotional distress of divorce is caused by the vesting of too much power in the hands of the female and her attorney, the new laws will go a long way towards increasing these powers with the inevitable consequences.

(author's italics)